What people have to say
and writing on the subj

MW01535240

"Chris Sutton has hit a homerun with his C.O.B.R.A. Self-Defense System. The program is highly effective, but at the same time easy to learn so anyone can participate. There are only two proven ways to attract a wide variety of adults into martial arts schools: fitness and self-defense. Of all the self-defense programs I've seen, C.O.B.R.A. is the best at attracting large numbers of adults who would otherwise never walk into a martial arts school."

   – Jim Graden, World Kickboxing Champion & Creator
     of the Ultimate Body Shaping Course

"The C.O.B.R.A. experience was very similar to what I taught as a combatives instructor for the United States Army. Chris Sutton's C.O.B.R.A. course teaches a suite of skills that can absolutely be used in any type of life-threatening situation. Personally I had my two daughters and two boys take the course because I am a big believer in the confidence it builds and the skill set it provides."

   – Sean Mitchner, Former Army Ranger/West Point Grad

"The C.O.B.R.A. Self-defense program was one of the best investments I have made in my life. I really enjoyed these classes because I feel like I will be able to have control if I am ever put in a situation. I'm not a big person, but I have confidence, power, and knowledge to defend myself."

   – Katie Harrison

"Chris Sutton is a great martial artist, friend and, in my opinion, a pioneer in street combat and self-defense for the non-martial artist. His program helps those not looking to be a martial artist but secure in their safety - he has done what many have failed to do. Having both the martial skill and the professional knowledge from his last profession, his class is something that no person or professional martial arts academy can truly do without."

   – Sifu Brian, Wing Chun Kung Fu Institute / PCSO Deputy

"An absolute asset to any female willing to develop sufficient attitude for survival."

   – Maxine Sutcliffe

"C.O.B.R.A. validated my strengths and exposed my weaknesses in all areas - I absolutely loved the program."

   – Corey Tramell, Professional Fitness Instructor

"This course made me realize just how little I knew! With C.O.B.R.A. training, even the smallest person can defend themselves."

    – Mike Eagle, Design Engineer

"The instructor's dedication to the course made it easy for me to achieve my goal in self-defense."

    – Carey Fortmuller

"It made me feel empowered and a lot more confident as a single female."

    – Natalie Wilbanks

"The things I learned in the C.O.B.R.A. course are invaluable. They may potentially save my life!"

    – Sara Gellatly

"This is a great course! I think my children will know how to react if they are in a dangerous situation. This is a great class for anyone!"

    – Pam Bass

"This program is vital to take! I am more conscious of my environment and don't put myself in dangerous areas. This program will teach you reality-based information that karate won't!"

    – Jamie Langford, Student

"I can't believe I went without self-defense training for 26 years! The training academy is AMAZING! You won't believe what simple techniques can be done to help defend yourself if you were in a bad situation!"

    – Amy Rench, Studio Manager

"I have been around the self-defense industry for over 15 years. This program has increased my skill level like no other program, plus it's fun!"

    – Mike Shultz, Tampa Police/Iraq War Vet

THE PSYCHOLOGY *of*
SELF-DEFENSE

THE PSYCHOLOGY *of* SELF-DEFENSE

How to Cultivate a
Superior Survival Mindset
for Today's World

CHRISTOPHER SUTTON

CES PUBLISHING
CLEARWATER, FLORIDA

THE PSYCHOLOGY OF SELF-DEFENSE -

How to Cultivate a Superior Survival Mindset for Today's World
by Christopher Sutton

CES Publishing

24103 U.S. Hwy. 19 N.
Clearwater, FL 33759 U.S.A.
Info@CobraDefense.com
http://www.cobradefensesystem.com

Unattributed quotations are by Christopher Sutton.

ISBN Softcover 978-0-615-27015-9

Library of Congress Catalog Card Number 2008912014

Printed in the United States of America

This book is dedicated to my family, my wife Shannon, and especially my son, Evan. He inspires me every second of every day. I love you, son.

- ACKNOWLEDGEMENTS -

For the help, inspiration and experience I've gained over the many years, I would like to thank all those who have contributed, both directly and indirectly. (I apologize if I've forgotten anyone.) So here goes...

I would like to thank all of my martial arts family and those who have contributed over my many years of training, including Jim Graden, Joe Lewis, and John Graden; all of my martial arts and self-defense students in the United Martial Arts Academy and the C.O.B.R.A. Self-Defense System; and all my Black Belts. I'd also like to thank all the law enforcement officers and DT instructors for the years of quality training and great experiences – especially George Walters.

For the creation of this project, I would like to thank Julie Gallagher, of gallaghercopywriting.com, for her professionalism and attention to detail, and Niki Vintson for all her contributions. I would also like to thank Theresa Brown, an author and the mother of my first Black Belt, Gabe Brown, for her many years of support and feedback.

I would especially like to thank my immediate family, Shannon and Christopher "Evan" Sutton (the young warrior): Thank you for your years of patience, support, ideas and input – thank you so much! I cannot thank you guys enough for everything you have done for me.

Lastly, I want to thank my father, Raymond Sutton: You were my best friend and a huge inspiration to me. You are missed.

Thank you for everything and I hope you enjoy the book!!

It has long been my belief that self-defense should be a prerequisite at some point in every person's life, preferably in their early years. It should be as normal as going to math class or learning to use a cell phone. Do you remember back when cell phones were as big as a lunch box, and only a few people had them? Now it's hard to imagine life without them. That's where we need to be as a society in regards to self-defense.

Throughout this book we'll discuss topics that most people ignore, forget, or overcomplicate. The object is not to put you in fear or stir up paranoia, but to educate you and create much-needed awareness and understanding.

I start with the basics, for beginners and intermediate students of self-defense. Later I also devote several chapters to experienced martial artists and others interested in martial philosophy.

This isn't a picture book about how to kick and punch. It's more a manual that seeks to sharpen the mind. This information can be applied by people of all ages, from all walks of life and all fitness levels.

You may read something here that shakes you up, frightens you, or even offends you. If that happens, please remember the goal: a no-ego, highly informative approach to give you, the reader, a look deep inside the psychology of self-defense and the creation of personal safety awareness and understanding.

Let me briefly introduce myself. My name is Chris Sutton, and I'm a professional in the self-defense and martial arts industry. I've also worked extensively as a corrections officer, a law enforcement officer, and a sheriff's deputy for city and county agencies. During my law enforcement years, I also served as a boot camp drill instructor for high-priority juvenile offenders.

From an early age, I've devoted a lot of time and effort to training in and instructing a wide variety of martial arts and combative self-defense programs, earning numerous black belts. I've dedicated my life to creating a greater awareness of self-defense training for everyone.

Drawing on both my diverse martial arts background and my practical experience in related fields, I developed the C.O.B.R.A. Self-Defense System, upon which this book is based. This nationally licensed self-defense program was designed to be highly effective, easy to learn, and very realistic.

Think of it this way: When you're hungry, you want food. Nothing else will satisfy you. Likewise, when you're in a serious situation, you need life-saving self-defense and awareness skills. Humor, a college degree, good looks – these won't cut it. "When self-defense is a must" ™ – nothing else will do. Think about this.

Ready? Let's get started!

Real-Life Self-Defense

"Training your body will cultivate your mind, exposing qualities and advantages no one can 'just get.' This will bring an understanding that what is gained carries more value and use than just for physical combat."

CHAPTER 1

This Is Reality

When confronted by the unknown, a person who is not physically and mentally prepared can suffer from and be paralyzed by fear – primal fear. Fear can be the last thing you feel before a tragedy or death. Denial, panic and fear can stop you in your tracks. Being prepared by learning realistic self-defense and knowing how to react in a stressful situation can be a priceless asset.

Ask yourself this question: Who will be there for you in a crisis situation? The answer is, YOU. When reality hits, it's unexpected, and you're usually alone. This can be a dreadful feeling, especially if you don't know what to do.

Let's be perfectly clear about one thing: You don't have to live in a heightened state of paranoia to achieve security in your life. You don't need an electric fence, armed guards, and attack pit bulls to get a good night's rest. You do need to be prepared.

We live in a great country with many laws in place to protect us. But a bad guy doesn't care about that, or about you.

Read the following paragraph very carefully:

The worst thing that could possibly happen to you probably won't happen. We live in a relatively safe society. You probably won't get sick from pesticides on unwashed fruit or salmonella in undercooked poultry, based on proven statistics.

Are you ok with the words "probably," "possibly," "could," and "relatively" in this example? Most individuals would never eat unwashed fruit or raw chicken, because of the "possibility" that they "could" get sick. On the other hand, most of those same people have never even thought about seeking an education on personal safety or anything related to it. This doesn't make them wrong, or a bad person in any way. It's just never been a priority for them.

You cannot rely on wishful thinking, religion, good luck, or hearsay. You must be proactive in obtaining security in life. Do it for yourself, your family, and your future.

A realistic conflict has its own feel, energy, fear, apprehension, and lasting mark on your mind. Trying to grasp something this intense when you have never experienced or trained for it is like trying to explain the color red to a person who has been blind their entire life. So I'll illustrate with a story. I won't divulge whether or not this particular incident really happened, or who it happened to – that isn't relevant – but I would like you as the reader to try to experience and live this story.

The Fight

A knowledgeable and competent man (we'll call him Scott) is speaking with a less-than-honorable and very malicious man (we'll call him John). Scott feels a surge of heat as blood rushes to his head. He looks up and realizes that John is slowly closing the four-foot gap between them. Scott gives a loud and commanding shout to John to not get any closer, but there is zero concern in John's face.

After an intense verbal altercation, Scott moves to physically gain control over John. Scott observes a passiveness about John that appears to be false. The two men are an inch apart, and as Scott is attempting to gain quick tactical control over John, his instincts set off every panic alarm in his body, even though John is being very passive.

Scott realizes that even though John is facing away and very calm, something is not right. John's knees are bent ever so slightly, and his chin is tilted to the side so his right eye is fixed on Scott.

Scott tastes enamel in his mouth from clenching his jaw so tightly. His hearing is dull but his eyesight is sharpened, and he notices a strong smell of car fumes, leather, and sweat. Scott has been here before and realizes he needs to breathe and focus, because he is now inside the energy of John, and they both understand what is about to take place.

Scott focuses past the darkness and the lights to see one bead of sweat on the right side of John's face. Scott and John lock eyes as John takes a deep breath. As Scott controls John's right wrist, John spins around fast, swinging the back of his left arm at Scott. Scott felt this coming right before it happened, and is prepared with his hands up next to his head. Scott is struck on the side of his head, but shielded by his own arm.

John begins to shout and curse, and attempts another strike. Scott realizes he won't have any help anytime soon, and remembers a truck honking as it drove by. Scott strikes John, and as John falls, Scott vividly remembers seeing a car entering a drive thru at a restaurant across the street.

John falls flat on his back, like in a movie, but he's getting up quick. Scott feels exceptionally calm and clear-headed because he has felt like this before.

John is fighting like a wild animal. Scott strikes John eight times, twice while he's against a car, and six more times as they are on the ground. Scott is on top and continues to strike John with a closed fist, elbows, and an open hand. John, in a fetal position, pulls his legs in and begins to roll over to attempt to stand up. Scott continues with knee strikes, so many he can't keep count.

The two men pause, tangled against a car. There's blood all over John's shirt and Scott's hands, and there is a distinct bloody drag mark on the car. Scott feels like he's stepped in water, because his feet are soaked with sweat. Scott's clothes are in disarray, and both men are breathing hard and sweating profusely.

John stands up and strikes Scott, hitting the side of his neck, then attempts to tackle him to the ground. Scott goes to the ground and is on top again. The fight continues, with Scott punching the ground while attempting to hit John. Scott can now taste and feel a rush of endorphins in his body. This is the third such shot he's felt since the outset of this conflict.

Scott begins to strike so fast he feels sick, but still he keeps going. John grabs the weapon Scott is carrying, and tries with all his might to get it from him. Scott reaches for John's eyes, clipping his right eye with his right index finger. John's eyes shut, but he's still fighting.

Scott stands up. He can't feel his legs very well. His throat is bone dry. John can't keep his grip due to the sweat and blood, and remains on the ground. Scott has never been where he is right now; everything has changed.

It's like a very bad dream – the kind of dream were you can't get out of the middle of a busy road. Scott is using all he's learned and everything he has. He hasn't sustained any real damage, however the feeling he's experiencing is uncharted territory. Scott can feel the damage he's inflicting on John, yet John keeps fighting.

John stands up and runs at Scott, and the two men lock up again. Scott picks up John and slams him to the ground as hard as he can. Scott begins to ask himself, "How much longer? Why is he not stopping after everything I've done to him?"

John attempts to choke Scott, but ends up just holding onto his shirt. Scott postures up, holds John by his throat, and begins to strike him repeatedly. Scott's arms are numb.

As both men again mutually pause in the heat of combat, Scott vividly sees his watch, which is approximately ten inches away as he's gripping John's neck. Scott knows what time the incident was initiated because his cell phone screen displayed the exact time as he got off his phone. It has only been fifty-seven seconds since this all began. It feels like thirty minutes to Scott. It's unreal.

To shorten the story, let's jump ahead...

Scott and John continued fighting for another seven minutes and thirty seconds. Although Scott didn't suffer any major physical damage, after it was over his body felt wrecked and his mind was on fire. John was physically much worse off, but it didn't really matter to him.

Scott learned many empowering and priceless things on that day.

Now let's go back to you, the reader. Would you like to experience ten, twenty, or thirty seconds of that story? Probably not. But it's not up to you. The bad guy picks the day, not you. What would you do if it happened today? How would you fare?

This book was written to give you a basic understanding of mental and physical self-defense/martial arts tactics.

Read, re-read, and completely understand this material. I cannot overstate this enough.

Welcome to the world of reality self-defense and its fundamental principles.

CHAPTER 2

The Importance of Self-Defense

When it comes right down to it, nobody in this world matters as much as you!

No one has a right to steal your possessions, your future, or your potential – bottom line. In that sense, you need to see yourself as the most important person in the world. You only live once, and you should try to be here as long as possible. I can't stand the stories about some pathetic thug who took the life of a mother of three. This is an absolute atrocity. She was a very important person; he was not.

Some of you might think this sounds selfish. I know you probably care a lot about your family, your friends, and so on. But think of it this way: what good are you to them if you're gone or hurt? When you keep yourself safe, secure, and healthy, you're making the people in your life who care about you happier, too.

My mission is to empower and educate as many individuals as possible to realize that they are each the most important person in this world, and to give them the skills with which to secure their lives for years to come. I truly believe that if you realize how important you really are, you will take steps to protect your life.

Let's look at the priorities in our society.

When you're at a shopping center and you make a major purchase – let's say an appliance, or even a new iPod – the individual across the counter asks, "Would you like to put insurance on this? It's only 16 (or 30, or 40) dollars a year." And a lot of us will say, "Yes, absolutely."

When you purchase a new car, you can't even leave the lot without purchasing a comprehensive insurance policy, which may cost thousands of dollars per year. Why? If you took out a loan to purchase the car, the bank or finance company wants to be sure they're protected. And you'll sleep better, too, knowing that if anything happens to your new toy, it will be replaced, or at least repaired properly. It's all about peace of mind.

Do you buy auto insurance because you plan to jump into this new vehicle and ram it into a wall or another car? Of course not. You buy it because you know you're going to be on the road with a lot of other drivers, and you never know which of those other drivers might be under the influence, or just not paying attention, and run into you.

It's the same when you buy a home. The bank won't complete the loan process until you purchase the proper insurance policy, because they want to make sure their investment is protected. And even though you hope nothing catastrophic is ever going to happen to your home, it's worth it to you to know you're covered – just in case.

In short, we go to great lengths to protect all the material objects in our lives. So why is our personal safety up for grabs?

Why don't we have self-defense training in the school system? From an early age you send your children to school, where they are taught many things. You name it, and there's a class on it – art, home economics, math, English, and so on. And while all these classes are certainly important, why is there no requirement to take a class on situational awareness and real self-defense?

It should be mandatory that your child will sit down and crack open a book and learn about who the bad guy is, what he thinks, and what can he do to you. That he's not the guy in the dark alley with the long trench coat, he's not the boogieman, and he's not the guy you see on TV. That the bad guy looks just like you and me.

And what about you? Since you weren't required to take a self-defense class in school, how about now? Surely as intelligent, mature adults we realize that we need to be able to protect ourselves. Right?

Did you know that the average woman will spend more on her hair and nails in one year than she will spend on personal safety in her entire lifetime? That many families spend more on rental movies in one year that they would ever spend on ten years of self-defense classes? Tactical training and martial arts fall at the very bottom of most people's priority list. We want to insure our material items – our cars, our houses, and everything around us – but when it comes to our own safety, we do nothing.

Why is that?

How *do* we rationalize what is and isn't important?

We live in a society where we see crime in the news every day, we read about it in the newspapers, and we hear about it from others – and yet somehow we don't wake up each morning and spend the whole day looking over our shoulders.

Please understand, I'm not saying that you have to be paranoid to be heads-up about self-defense, personal safety, and situational awareness. Paranoia isn't a part of the mindset of self-defense. The point is, instead of learning from the experience of others, we tend to disassociate ourselves from the people we see or read about in the news, because we don't know them. We haven't attached ourselves to them emotionally, so they're not real to us. We think, "That couldn't happen to *me*."

We hope and believe that we can always put ourselves in the right place, and that someone will always be there for us. We gloss over the fact that maybe the victim on the news was in a good neighborhood, drove a nice car, made a lot of money, and didn't know their attacker, and yet still became the victim of this brutal individual. Instead we go on fixing dinner, or whatever else we're doing, and we don't give it a second thought.

Think about this: On a daily basis, who do you interact with? Other people. You come into contact with hundreds if not thousands of people every year, and you don't know ninety-five percent of them. From the time you get up until the time you go to bed, you interact with other human beings. And what is the source of the threat when it comes to self-defense? Other human beings. Yet when it comes to crime, most people prefer to look the other way and hope for the best. How does that make sense?

Once you've been in a situation, hindsight is 20/20. That's when you begin to say stuff like, "I wish I would have taken a class. Well, this is never going to happen to me again. I'm going to get a concealed weapons permit. I'm going to take martial arts. I'm going to take a self-defense class."

If you knew ahead of time that you were going to become a victim, you would probably act to prevent it. That's why we're going to go one more step. I want you to just stay with me, please, while I take you on a little journey.

Imagine you have the ability to time travel. You're going to go ahead two years (or six months, or one year -- it doesn't really matter). When you get there you're going to open up a newspaper or search the Internet, and you're going to find that either you or someone very close to you became the victim of a brutal crime. Maybe they were robbed, maybe they were murdered, maybe they were raped, maybe they were brutalized to the point where they were handicapped or it caused some kind of emotional distress that they're going to live with for the rest of their life.

Then, because you have the ability to time travel, you come back to today. Knowing what's going to happen, how much will you spend to seek out self-defense training? What will you be willing to do to tip the scales in your favor, and change the outcome that you witnessed in the future?

Obviously none of us can time travel (that I know of). But by doing this exercise, you can imagine what it would be like if you went into the future, and you found out that your mom was robbed and beaten. They took her car and left her for dead, and she didn't make it. And you can ask yourself what you could have done to change that.

Now say you couldn't just stop her before she went out to the car – that you can't change time like that. But you *could* empower her with knowledge. Maybe she didn't park in a well-lit parking area. Maybe she was jingling her keys. Maybe she left her car unlocked when she got in because she began to adjust the mirror. Or she was looking for something in the console. Or she made a phone call. Whatever it was, she stayed in the parking lot twenty-five seconds too long, which gave an individual who scouted her out because she was the last one leaving the opportunity to walk across the parking lot, open the car door, and carry out the plan that he wanted to carry out.

The education that she could have gotten over the last six months, year, or two years could have saved her life.

She didn't have to become a prize fighter, and step out of the car and whoop this individual. That's not what we're looking for. Because remember, self-defense isn't about whooping somebody – it's about surviving. You can beat someone to a bloody pulp, and you don't get a title belt. You don't get a trophy. You don't get ten seconds on the news half the time.

On the other hand, if you lose – if they take your life, if they victimize you – you *might* get a ten-second spot on the news. But who's destroyed? Everyone in your family. Everyone close to you. And everything you ever worked for is gone at the hands of some thug, some criminal who made his plan just because he thought you were a weak target.

You have to realize and understand that it can happen to anyone. So let's just go ahead and time travel, all right? Do this exercise for me and it will definitely open up your mind and expand what you think about as far as the potential hazards in this world.

Does this mean that if you take a self-defense class, you'll never become a victim? Absolutely not. And if there's an instructor or an organization or a program out there that preaches, "If you do this, you will always be safe" or "If you do this move you will always win" – that's nonsense. We're talking about a ninety percent effectiveness rate. That's a reasonable goal when it comes to protecting ourselves, our loved ones, and our families.

It can be absolutely anything, from the lowest priority of self-defense to the highest priority, from a bullying situation to a weapon involved, from a domestic situation to a multiple attacker situation. It really doesn't matter. Education is of the utmost importance.

Self-defense knowledge is lifesaving. I wish the kids had it. I wish the young females had it. I wish the young males had it – especially the guys who walk around thinking, "You know what? I'm a pretty in-shape guy. I took a couple of boxing classes. There's no way anyone's going to victimize me."

Hey guys, guess what – you might have a very nice car and two guys with a long rap sheet are across the street staring at you. Maybe they're on probation. Maybe they broke out of jail. Maybe they just don't care. They've put the bull's-eye on you, and they're planning to take your very nice car. They'll do whatever they have to do to get it, and then drive it all over the county, or all over the state, and just joy ride. And if you're in their way, guess what – you're the victim.

It really doesn't matter whether you're in shape, or you're not in shape. You can insure your life to the hilt with just general education and knowledge. You don't have to be hitting a bag all the time. You don't have to say, "I can do a hundred and fifty push-ups in twenty seconds and hit a bag harder than anyone." That has nothing at all to do with reality training. (I'll discuss this further in the section on Combat Conditioning – how what you do in an enclosed, controlled environment doesn't translate very well at all once you're out there.) It's not about street fighting, because most fights don't happen in the middle of the street. It's about real-life situational training and self-defense.

Let's not be reactive; let's be proactive. This is empowering. Instead of only insuring our cars, refrigerators, and iPods, let's start thinking about ourselves. Yes, we need car insurance and home insurance and even nice hair and nails – but don't forget how important self-defense and personal safety education are in today's society. Even one class or seminar can be empowering and life saving. Overall, it's a very small investment to protect your biggest asset – YOU!

Zero Training? Read this

No self-defense training? All the more reason to start a training program, read this book, or start a martial art. Think of it like this: You've been driving around your most valuable asset (you) uninsured your entire life. What are you worth? If you had to put a price tag on yourself, what would it be? Priceless, right? It's so important to make self-defense training a priority, and it's never too late.

CHAPTER 3

What is Real-Life Self-Defense

This is a topic that has been debated forever.

The question "What is real self-defense?" prompts many to play their ego card. Some people become emotional and personally offended at the suggestion of anything outside their world. This attitude in itself puts others in harm's way, and keeps the majority of the general public in the dark when it comes to receiving a real, life-saving education. Therefore, I promise not to impose my opinion, favoritism, or ego in this book, but rather to base what I say on facts and high-percentage, proven statistics.

The average person's idea of what constitutes "self-defense training" is generally the furthest thing from the truth. Although there are many ways to describe reality self-defense, most people's views, opinions, and beliefs about what it takes to protect themselves are heavily influenced by TV shows, poor trainers, hearsay, and Hollywood fighting such as wrestling.

Try to wipe the slate clean of any outside influence as you read this chapter. Read it several times if that helps you build a solid vision of what it takes to survive.

The real definition of self-defense is: **the ability to avoid conflict and/or to adequately defend yourself in a conflict**. You must be able to do this under extreme stress and fear. In a real-life situation there are no rules, no refs, no controlled environments, and, most likely, no help. Your attacker will always pick the time, place, and method of attack; you will never get this luxury. No matter what the outcome, you won't receive a trophy, title belt, or medal of valor.

What does it take to spark a real-life attack or conflict? As little as a look – sometimes even less. Usually, your attacker won't know you. He won't care how much money you have, how important you are, how much you love your family, or about anything else in your world. You will be nothing but an opportunity for him. That's why the first part of the definition of self-defense – **the ability to avoid conflict** – is so important.

Opportunity Knocks

When a potential attacker seeks his prey, he looks for basically one thing: OPPORTUNITY.

Think about the decision-making process of the average person. Humans thrive on opportunity in all things. Here are some examples:

- You park in the closest open spot to the store
  instead of across the lot
- You invest when asset prices are down to make
  more money
- You save money by shopping when there's a sale
- You get a college education to expand your options
- You apply for the highest paying job available
- You would cut in line at Disney World, if they'd
  let you

I could go on and on, and so could you. The point is, it's the same with self-defense. Whatever opportunity you give, someone might take.

Imagine a fortress. Now think like an attacker for a minute. Are the gates locked? Are the walls too high? Are there guards, dogs, or rivers to cross? Did someone see you coming and sound an alarm? If your chances of success are low, you'll probably move on, because there's always a softer target right down the road.

This is how a potential attacker evaluates you.

Proactive Situational Awareness

When we drive down a street, we look ahead for people pulling out in front of us, objects in the road, traffic signals, and so on. When we first learned how to drive, most of us were so nervous we couldn't see past the hood of our car. This is known as "tunnel vision." Now driving is second nature. Our minds have been conditioned to handle all this without stressing out.

Likewise, we can train ourselves to process information about people, places, and events, and to formulate proactive responses that can prevent dangerous situations from developing. This ability to foresee and avoid trouble without becoming paranoid, learned through realistic self-defense training and education, can also become second nature. This kind of proactive situational awareness is a priceless asset to anyone.

But what if, for some reason, you can't avoid a dangerous situation? That's when the second part of the definition – ...**or to adequately defend yourself in a conflict** – comes into play.

Your Single Greatest Weapon

To access your skill, knowledge, decision making ability, and awareness, you absolutely have to have the following: *a brain!* The good news is, if you're reading this, you probably have one.

Your brain houses all the controls for any and all actions in your life, especially when it comes to survival and self-defense. Without tapping into your mental ability, your physical ability – despite training – is mediocre at best. I hope I'm not overstating the obvious. I'm trying to shed light on a topic most people ignore.

Intense physical self-defense training done without the element of reality leaves most people in better shape, but still unable to adequately defend themselves. Why? They haven't been introduced to or received education in **reality** self-defense.

Real-life conflicts are nothing like what we see on TV, in sports, or in movies. It's not even close. The tragedy is, without professional training, this is the only frame of reference most people will ever have.

That's why reality self-defense training is so important. It links mind and body together, to create maximum effectiveness.

Controlling Fear and Panic

When facing a real-life situation that could prove dangerous or even fatal, most people panic and freeze in their tracks.

When we're overcome by fear and panic, our mental and physical abilities become greatly impaired. Have you ever been really nervous about an upcoming event, such as playing in a sporting event, or giving a big speech at work? If so, you know how it can put you on edge, or even fill you with fear. Now imagine being in a situation where your life literally hangs in the balance. Under such circumstances, fear can be paralyzing. If you don't learn how to control it, your whole life can change in a second.

Fear and panic never completely go away – nor do you want them to. But by controlling our fear, we can use it to our advantage. When properly channeled, fear heightens your senses during a confrontation. It can also increase your strength and improve your reaction time.

What's affected during a conflict?

• Vision
• Hearing

- Decision making ability
- Perception of time
- Memory
- Pain Perception
- Balance and Control
- Voice inflection

With training and experience you can access and use the effects of fear to your advantage instead of letting them impair your ability to function.

So how do we control fear and panic? It's not something you can learn in a classroom setting. It takes repeated applications of stress to build up your nervous system and break down those paralyzing barriers. Realistic martial arts and self-defense training can help you deal with, and adjust to, fear and panic.

Imagine going to a gun range for the first time. You're at the front desk, and although you're aware of where you are, you jump and become nervous when you hear the gunshots. Then you notice that the employees and regular customers go about their business like it's no big deal. After a while, it won't be a big deal to you, either.

Or how about the first time you rode a roller coaster? You were probably filled with fear and at the edge of your seat. As you rode the coaster repeatedly, your senses and nervous system eventually adjusted to the situation, and you probably found yourself wanting to figure out where the cameras are so you could smile for them.

Reality training has the same effect. When you train in a realistic manner, your body and mind will remember, and be prepared to react appropriately whenever you're in a real-life altercation. You'll still experience fear and anxiety, but because of the training you've received, you'll be able to work through it instead of shutting down. You'll be in control of your emotions and actions during a crisis, which will give you the upper hand in any situation.

The goal of scenario-based training is to give you the ability to make your fear your fuel. Let fear be a warning that prepares you, not an emotion that overwhelms you.

CHAPTER 4

Common Misconceptions that Can Get You Killed

I'm sure you've heard this conversation (or one like it) before:

"I'm in martial arts."

"I don't need martial arts. I have a .357. Ha! What are you going to do about *that*?"

This is a very common misconception: If you own a gun, you're all set to protect yourself. But to anyone with any degree of reality-based training, that statement would be laughable if it weren't so dangerous.

People say things like that out of ignorance. And it's not really their fault. They don't know any better. It's maybe what they saw on TV. Or they think just having a gun gives them a lot of power. But just because even a two-year-old can shoot somebody, that doesn't make the gun all-powerful.

Yes, many people have been killed by guns – including many gun owners with a concealed weapons permit, who ended up getting killed with their own weapon. They pulled it, and then they didn't know how to use it. They didn't have the ability to get it out, aim it, and fire the round that would stop the threat. Why? Because, having never done it before, they shut down. So the bad guy took it away from them and used it instead. Even law enforcement officers, with all their training, are sometimes killed with their own weapon.

Just having a gun doesn't make anyone invincible.

As we will discuss in greater detail later in this book, you can shoot at a target all day long and hit bull's-eyes; but once you're in a shootout, everything changes. So the individual who says "I have a gun. I don't need any type of training" is speaking from ignorance.

Another reason why having a weapon may not be enough is that it takes far longer than you think to get a gun out and use it.

If you've ever attended one of our seminars or been in one of our classes – and there are many other self-defense courses out there which will show you the exact same thing – you've seen a demonstration of the reaction time of an individual when it comes to real-life self-defense, and what they can and cannot do. The results come as a surprise to most people.

We give one of the female students a training gun, and have her put it in a purse. We then ask her how many feet of distance from a bad guy she thinks she needs to be able to get the gun out and actually shoot the guy. They usually say, "Maybe five feet."

They never get it out it time. They don't even get the purse unzipped.

Then we have another student – male or female – put it in their waistband, and we ask them how many feet they need. They saw what happened before, so this time they say, "Fifteen feet."

They cannot get it out of their waistband. Ninety-nine percent of the people can't get it out of their waistband fast enough. And even when they do, they don't draw down and pull the trigger.

Then we put it in their hands, and we go to point blank. They cannot, in a struggle, get the gun up to perfect a shot.

We can be thirty-five feet away, and *walk* to them, and if that gun is in a bag, we get to them before they can get it out. They're too confused, they're too overwhelmed, and they simply cannot do it. Even with a lot of training, many individuals can't get their weapon out fast enough.

So say you have a concealed weapons permit, and your gun is in your glove compartment, and you think, "Well, you know, I've got that gun. I feel pretty safe." And then all of a sudden someone comes up and grabs your hair and tries to rip you out of you car. The likelihood of your using that gun for it's intended purpose is very low. You'll never get to it, much less get a shot off.

A bad guy can be twenty-one feet away with a knife in his hand, and he'll stab you before you can get your gun out. That's what the studies show, that's the statistics, and that's what testing has proven time and time again.

The same thing applies to a cell phone. A lot of people think they're safe because they carry a cell phone. If something happens, they'll just call 911, and the police will come save them. But this is another dangerous misconception.

A while back we did a fifteen-minute segment on a local morning show here in Florida, in which we demonstrated this. The drill went like this: "Put this phone in your bag. I'm going to stand as far away as I possibly can. As soon as I start to move, go after the phone. All I want you to do is unzip the bag, get the phone out, dial 911, and describe to the operator what I look like, where you're at, and that you're in trouble."

We tested it over and over and over again with different people – regular people, both children and adults. The individual could never get their cell phone out, no matter how much room we gave them. Twenty-five feet, thirty-five feet, forty-five feet. The stage wasn't big enough.

Now, keep in mind, this person knew we were coming. We told them we were coming, and no, we didn't sprint to them. They knew exactly where the phone was, and they had prepared themselves for this. They could not get the phone out. I believe one time someone got the phone out – and then dropped it. Never was 911 dialed correctly.

We did this many times, with many different people, and every one got stuck in what we call the "goofy loop" (hypervigilance). They got shut down by their own adrenaline. And I'm not even a real bad guy. This was just from being tasked to get the cell phone out with people watching.

Suppose you do manage to get your phone out and dial 911. What then? You've got to tell the dispatcher what's happening, where you are, and give a complete description of your attacker. Then you have to wait for the authorities to arrive.

Think about this: The police are three, or five, or ten minutes away. The bad guy is already on the scene. Do you want to spend ten, or five, or even three minutes with a bad guy? He can kill you in twenty seconds or less.

Cell phones do have their place. If your car breaks down in a remote area, being able to stay with your car and call for roadside assistance is much safer than having to walk along the highway searching for help. But don't let yourself be lulled into a false sense of security because you were misinformed by someone who told you to put all your stock in that little electronic device. The results could be tragic.

In short, it's dangerous to believe you can do something when you really can't. You can't protect yourself like you think you can with a gun, especially if you're untrained. Using your cell phone to dial 911 won't save you if you don't have the luxury of time. You can't learn how to kick and punch appropriately just from reading a book. You can't learn what you need to know to defend yourself by listening to your friends or watching a movie.

But there are also a lot of things that you probably believe you can't do that you actually can. With the proper training, you can learn techniques that are effective in the kinds of situations we're talking about. For example, you'll learn that action beats reaction every time, and you can use that to your advantage. You'll learn that in a knife fight, you will most likely get cut – because it's incredibly difficult to stop an edged weapon – but it's *where* you get cut that's important. (Getting cut on your arms is okay. Getting cut in your abdomen or neck or low back is not.)

The important thing is to do your homework. Know what you can do. Know what absolutely doesn't work. Be sure to seek out correct, effective tactical information from a professional source. In Appendix B, I give a list of resources you might want to consult for further information. Or simply shop around in your own area. There are a wide variety of instructors, schools and establishments out there that are willing to teach you this.

In writing this book, I have no bias for one martial art over another. I am, however, a big advocate of making sure self-defense information is communicated correctly, with the best interests of the student in mind. Therefore I recommend that you carefully read the chapters "How to Pick a Martial Arts School or Self-Defense Program" and "The Difference Between Self-Defense and Martial Arts" to further guide you in your selection.

C H A P T E R   4

The Truth About Child Safety and Defense

When it comes to safety and self-defense for children 3-12 years old, there are a couple of things that need to be noted.

First, what true child safety *isn't*. It's not about striking a bag, performing kicks, breaking boards, or sparring in tournaments. This is as true for children as it is for adults.

Most children receive zero formal education in real situational awareness and self-defense. Generally all they receive are basic classes on hitting a bag, if they're lucky.

The idea of at least getting them into a martial arts class is good. But to make sure that what they learn will be useful to them in the real world, you, the parent, must research the instructor's qualifications, the degree of reality experience in the program, and the teaching methods. (We'll cover more on this in the next chapter, "How to Pick a Martial Arts School or Self-Defense Program.")

What true child safety and self-defense are about is a soft target – a child – up against a full-grown attacker, usually a male.

What makes a child a soft target? They're shorter, lighter, and weaker than the average adult. They can't employ great leverage, which means they don't have the ability to take down or manipulate joints or anything like that. They're also highly impressionable. They're not naturally aggressive. They don't usually get into using functional weapons or carrying weapons on them.

Their strikes may be good against a schoolyard bully, but not against a full-grown attacker. A child twelve years old or under cannot execute a technique effectively against a full-grown attacker. When I say execute a technique, I mean they can't punch or kick their way out of a fight. Bottom line. We've tested this over and over in our organization, the C.O.B.R.A. Self-Defense Program.

Don't just take my word for it. Have you ever been hit by a ten-year-old's hardest punch? Whether you're a man or a woman, it won't ruin your day at all. Now imagine you're someone who has intent and motive to kidnap the child. If the child hits you, you're going to work through it, and you're going to keep right on fighting.

Now, having said that, there are many things a child *can* do to defend themselves. In our program we teach several different techniques, from anchoring, all the way to eye gouging and biting. These are highly effective techniques.

However, if you run into an instructor out there who tries to sell you on the idea that if your child punches a full-grown male in the stomach he will stop, or if she kicks him in his knee he will back off – it just does not happen. Almost physically impossible. The image of your child throwing, punching, or kicking her way out of a situation with an adult is just plain false. In fact, it's a recipe for disaster.

So remember, when looking for a child-safety-specific self-defense class, please keep these points in mind. There are a lot of good classes out there, but the truth about child safety and self-defense must be taken into consideration.

Ignorance Is Bliss – But It Can Also Be Deadly

Recently I was conducting a lesson on anti-abduction techniques at our national headquarters in Clearwater, Florida. Although kidnapping isn't reserved just for kids – women and men can be forcibly restrained and abducted as well – this particular seminar focused on children ages 7-13.

Through our many years of research, aggressive testing and re-testing (and yes, even more testing), we can confidently state what will be an effective technique in a certain situation. Effective doesn't mean fool-proof, of course – nothing is fool-proof in this world. Effective doesn't mean it looks good, or even that it's common practice. It just means that there's a really good chance that it will work.

For this lesson we were outside in the parking lot. I was reviewing an anchoring technique, in which a person wraps their arms around the window frame of the abductor's vehicle. You know the frame of your car door, if the window is down? Can you picture it? You slide your arms through and grab close to your elbows, which keeps the door from shutting.

One of the mothers who was watching became concerned. "If my daughter wraps around that frame, what if the kidnapper slams the door really hard?" she asked. "Or what if he drives off and she gets dragged down the street – falls – breaks her arm?"

Inside my head I got upset at this lady for not knowing right from wrong for her daughter, and for having a mindset that could get her or her daughter killed. On the outside, I listened. My inner dialog went quiet. Then I began thinking, It's my fault. She's not supposed to know something she's never been taught.

So, because I'm passionate about my profession, I seized the opportunity she gave me. I explained not only to her but to all the parents and kids who were there that day. I said:

"Ma'am, given the chance, which would you want? A: Your daughter is now in the back seat of this vehicle, because she did nothing to stop it. She's in the back seat of the kidnapper's car, it's locked, they're screaming down the highway at fifty to a hundred miles an hour, going to an unknown place, in a quiet, deserted area. Or B: Your daughter is taking the initiative to save her life and possibly falling down or breaking her arm or getting hurt in the process.

"Now your daughter's hurt – but within five to ten minutes an ambulance will show up and tend to her wounds, and professional medical staff will be waiting at the hospital to treat her injuries. She'll be taken very good care of. Most importantly, even though she's hurt, she's still alive and still with you.

"Or, you can see how well she fares with a kidnapper. Once they get to where they're going, I'm sure he'll be real accommodating to her. Ma'am, if that were the case, she would most likely be found a few days later, raped and dead. Possibly getting hurt trying to save her own life is the best thing that could happen to her in this situation.

"Many years of studying, training and experience tell me so. And many years of zero studying, training and experience are why you're asking me this question. Do we all understand?"

You could hear a pin drop, and everyone present nodded their head yes. The mother in question began to tear up, at which point I knew I had done my job.

I didn't want to just answer this caring mother's question about her daughter, I wanted to impact everyone present. I wanted to impact them like the meteor that wiped out the dinosaurs. That meteor made a massive difference. What I said and how I said it changed her mindset completely, along with the rest of the class.

She couldn't stop thanking me. But I was merely passing along facts and information from my experience. And I advised her to do the same. Because I made a difference in her life, hopefully she will go on and make a difference in many other's lives, and so on.

Remember, you don't know what you don't know. Ignorance is bliss, but it can be very deadly, as well.

CHAPTER 6

How to Pick a Martial Arts School or Self-Defense Program

Picking a school is easy. Picking the *right* school is smart, and a great investment.

I have no bias toward any particular art. I love all systems and arts, and I'll give you my reason why: The car you drive may carry the name Ford, or Nissan, or whatever. But in the end, despite all their little differences, all cars were made for one thing – to move you efficiently from point A to point B. Everything else is personal preference.

Martial arts are much the same. You can have a million styles or names, but in the end they all have a single focus: Enhancing your overall life.

But all martial arts schools are *not* the same.

Say you sign up for a martial arts class because you're sold on all the trophies and salesmanship of the owner/instructor/manager. You've been told that he trains with the best (though you never get details; just a name followed by "black belt this and that," which leads nowhere). You explain that your main objective is to learn real self-defense – techniques you can use in many different situations.

Your instructor says, "No problem. I am the East, West, North, and South Super Champion of the World in point sparring."

He then proceeds to teach you how to punch and kick to score points in a sports contest.

What's wrong with this picture?

Your instructor promised to teach you self-defense. But he's not qualified in this area. So instead you're learning how to score points in a sport in order to win a trophy. To top it off, you're very unsure of his credentials, his background, and his concern for your training.

If you want to learn a sport martial art, that's fine. Do that, and become good at it. But if you want reality self-defense, this scenario is a disaster. Many students walk out of their training facilities feeling a false sense of security because they were mislead.

Now, I'm probably not very good at point sparring, and I don't care to learn. But I also would never pretend that I *do* know about it, nor would I have the audacity to take on a student and try to teach it to them. It's like an English teacher trying to teach advanced physics – it just doesn't work.

So how do you choose the right school?

It really comes down to paying attention to how you feel when you meet an owner or walk into a school. You'll know you're in the right place the same way you know your shoes fit. It's that simple.

Here are some things to watch out for:

Beware of any instructor who:

- Has trophies everywhere as soon as you walk in
- Immediately talks about how great he or she is and shows little genuine interest in you
- Claims to be a "grandmaster" but is under 45 or 50 years old
- Has an answer for every question or move
- Gets defensive when you ask about credentials (this is the least they should produce)
- Claims their sport, sparring, or tournament award means they are qualified to teach reality self-defense
- Is an egomaniac (Beware! There are lots)
- Gives overly harsh critiques and shows a lack of

professional respect
- Has a title as long as your address
- Is self-taught (Yes, they are out there)
- Is an Internet "Black Belt" (Wow!)
- Anyone who won't shake your hand
- Is a money monster ("Sign here now! You want to learn this, right?")
- Is a self-proclaimed "street fighter" (Fights rarely happen in the streets)
- Does not have your best interest at heart
- Anyone who talks down about another system, art, or instructor (Whether they like them or not, they should be professional.)

If you notice any of these red flags, hold onto your wallet and run like you-know-what. Remember that you deserve the best when starting your martial arts and/or self-defense journey.

I'm a professional martial artist and school owner. Although I have many medals, awards, etc., I have not one trophy or picture of me in my training center. (Okay, I lied – I have a picture of me and my son. But that's different.)

Students know when you're a professional. You don't have to convince them. Having your credentials in an inconspicuous area is great, but it should not convey the feel of an overwhelming show of your ego.

Why is this important?

Your instructor is there for YOU, the student – to make you better, to educate you and add value to your life. That's the bottom line.

What to look for in an instructor:

- Professional
- Polite

- Informative
- Commonsense approach
- Willingness to help
- No high pressure
- Clean training area
- Solid background in what you seek

Remember, when you train as a martial artist, you gain more than you could ever imagine. After you've secured your self-defense skills, the martial arts begin to cultivate and enhance your entire life, body, and mind – so choose your school and instructors wisely.

"Practice is the only way you will ever come to understand what the way of the warrior is about. Constant striving for perfection of the self through a chosen art is the only path to enlightenment. Words can only bring you to the foot of the path; to attain mastery and perfection, you must constantly strive to better yourself through an understanding of your chosen way."

– Miyamoto Musashi, *The Book of Five Rings*, 1643

Know Your Enemy

"How do you feel about going into combat? Is your spirit correct at all times? Are you feeling strong? Do you feel slightly uneasy? It is important that you understand yourself with regard to the possibility of fighting. Another consideration is that the enemy has these thoughts as well. The better you know the opponent, the better equipped you are for battle. The skill you need for winning a battle lies in knowing the enemy's strengths and weaknesses. You achieve this through constantly practicing with the attitude to destroy the enemy. Knowing where you are at all times and understanding your relationship to the battle. Knowing the time means that you can instantly asses your situation and act accordingly. When you have acquired the correct attitude, you will be able to easily beat the enemy because you will be truly prepared to go into combat with an understanding of all the skills and abilities that you and your opponent possess."

– Miyamoto Musashi, *The Book of Five Rings*

Musashi lived in the 17th century, fighting for his life on a daily basis. He understood that the weakness of the enemy was his own weakness. The strength of the enemy could possibly be his own strength. So whatever strength he assigned to the enemy, whatever fear he had of the enemy – basically he was looking in a mirror. Whatever he saw in his enemy, he saw in himself. Human beings are all the same. We all have the same strengths and weaknesses. Musashi had it dead-on hundreds of years ago as a samurai.

CHAPTER 7

Scout the Other Team – Gather Intelligence

You are the good guy (or gal) – we have established that. Anyone formulating a plan to victimize, bully, or attack you is the bad guy. In this chapter, let's refer to the bad guys as "the other team."

To defend against the other team, you have to know the basics: How to recognize them, what they are capable of, and how they formulate plans. It's pretty straightforward, and should make sense to you.

What does the other team look like? Like you, your friends, or anyone else with two arms and two legs.

What does the other team think? That you can't win, that you have no skill and no heart, that you're afraid, that they're smarter than you, that they won't get caught, that their plan will work despite your best efforts.

Your objective is:

- To recognize a threat before it happens;
- To avoid conflict if at all possible;
- To actively defend yourself if conflict isn't avoidable; and
- To stop the threat at any and all costs.

What isn't at stake?

- Points
- Glory
- A trophy
- A title belt

What *is* at stake?

- Your mental stability
- Your material possessions
- Your financial worth
- Your pride
- Your life's work
- Your fun
- Your family
- Your future

What you lose in a confrontation with members of the other team could be as little as your watch, or as extreme as your life.

I don't know about you, but I'm not willing to give up my future, my family, and my life's work because of the actions of some dirt-bag thug. (If a person can't or won't get their act together, conform to today's society, and become a law abiding citizen, then, yes, I call them a dirt-bag thug. I don't care if they're wearing a suit and tie. I have more compassion for the ground I step on than for this type of person. If you have a hard time with this, then you've probably never met one of these people.)

Bad guys know they're bad guys. That's why they lie, steal and cover up. They run when in trouble, they fight when confronted, and they manipulate better than some Hollywood actors. Rarely do they change their ways. There are exceptions, but usually a vicious schoolyard bully will grow up to be a vicious adult bully, or much worse.

They will try to justify and rationalize who and what they are by saying they were picked on, beaten, abused, or from a broken home. But these are not valid excuses for victimizing others. Everyone has a story – everyone. I don't know about you, but I believe a bad childhood isn't a free pass to be a lawless villain, or even a petty thief.

So, why *do* some people choose to prey upon and victimize other people?

- Pride
- Pleasure
- Perversion
- Material gain
- Financial gain
- Revenge

This list isn't exhaustive, but you get the idea.

In the next chapter we're going to map out some of the common thought processes and actions of bad guys, to help you avoid becoming a victim.

CHAPTER 8

Criminal Intent

"Criminal intent" is defined here as the criminal thought process and motives pertaining to crime and violence. Criminals, thugs, punks, abusers – they're all part of the same "family," in that they generally think alike and carry out plans in similar ways.

Here are some quick facts on bad guys and their typical methods:

- The majority of criminals **do not** look the part. They look like everyone else.
- Being a criminal doesn't make you fearless. In fact, these "geniuses" are usually cowards who are just as afraid as those they attack.
- Bad guys prey on people they perceive as **"soft targets."**
- Most criminals are extremely lazy, and won't work hard at committing a crime.
- The easiest, fastest and least challenging way is what a bad guy looks for.
- The majority of bad guys flee or give up at the first hint of trouble or resistance.
- A lot of criminals take great pride in what they do.

- The phrase "like attracts like" is very true in the criminal world.
- Criminals don't expect much resistance from a victim; they rely on fear and intimidation to get the job done.
- Most bad guys have extremely poor plans, and usually no back up plans.
- Criminals can often be thrown out of sync very easily because they expect little or no resistance.
- Many of your everyday actions can determine whether or not you will become a target.
- Approximately five percent of the population commit the majority of all crimes.
- If you are *perceived* as strong, confident and posing a challenge, your chances of becoming a victim decrease dramatically.
- At some point in your life, you probably were the target of a crime and didn't even know it. The **smallest actions** you took prevented a bad guy from carrying out his plan.

These tips apply to the majority of crimes and criminals. However, every situation is unique and can possibly have a different outcome, so remember to stay alert and listen to your instincts.

CHAPTER 9

Threat Recognition

Recognizing a potential threat is eighty percent of the battle. You must be able to recognize a threat whether it's obvious or not.

Who is a threat? Anyone who is attempting to control you, deceive you, intimidate you, or cause you bodily harm. This includes anyone who lies, steals, scams, or attempts to victimize you in any way.

Anyone has the potential to be a threat to you, but it usually takes criminal intent for someone to follow through with violence or a crime. Men, women, teenagers, and even small children can harm you, but only if they intend to do so. You don't have to live your life in constant fear; you should, however, be alert for signs of criminal intent.

Pay attention to a person's actions, or lack thereof. When you get an uncomfortable feeling, this is a red flag – a signal that you may have a threat on your hands.

(Later in this book we'll talk about the three A's – Awareness, Alarm and Action. For now, it's important to note that once you are progressing through the three A's, your body is under stress. This is your body's natural security system, so listen to your gut!)

Here are some examples of situations that should make you think that something isn't right:

- A man wearing excessive clothing or a heavy jacket on a hot day (could be hiding a weapon)
- An unknown person knocking on your door claiming to be a repair or delivery person (could be a scam artist, a sexual predator, or scouting for burglary)
- A man who drives by an elementary school and stops to sit and watch the children as they leave (possible pedophile, molester or abductor)
- A person you remember arguing with earlier is now waiting outside the building as you're leaving (potential fight)
- Angry and aggressive significant other who is an extremist (possible domestic violence, murder, or mental abuse)
- Two people who approach you in a parking lot, talking fast, trying to sell you something or borrow money (possible scam, theft or robbery)
- Somebody you just met or have not known very long asks a lot of questions such as: Where do you live? Do you live with someone? Where do you work? When do you get home? When do you leave? Do you own a dog? (potential rapist, stalker, or murderer)
- Anyone who always offers to assist you with certain tasks, who generally doesn't do this for other people (may have an agenda)
- Someone you know who always wants to know your entire plan for the day, or who times your coming and going (possibly hiding something)
- Someone watching from their car in a parking lot (could be a car thief, a stalker, a set up for robbery – or someone who's just plain bored)

Any of these situations might turn out to be nothing. But it's better to be cautious about a situation and wrong, than to be careless and wrong.

There are many clues you can look for. You just need to pay attention to any signs, no matter how subtle. Again, listen to your gut! There's no harm in that – and it might save your life.

CHAPTER 10

Three Types of Bad Guys

Bad guys can be classified in many different ways. In this book, we're going to divide them into the three categories covered in the C.O.B.R.A. Self-Defense Program: the Bully, the Wolf, and the Predator. Let's look at each one of these types, and discuss how you can best deal with each of them.

The Bully

Bullies don't hide the fact that they're trying to boss you around, intimidate you, or threaten you. They generally have low self-esteem and use picking on others to feel better about their own life. A bully is generally not violent, relying instead on fear and intimidation to accomplish his or her goal. Bosses, friends, co-workers, family, and, of course, strangers can all be bullies.

How to Handle a Bully:

- Do not do what they want
- Get others involved (ask for help)
- Change your routine (avoid them)
- Travel with friends or family; be seen around others
- Get the authorities involved, if applicable

- When confronted, speak loudly and confidently
- Let the bully know that everyone knows what they're doing
- Never let them within your circle of security (your personal space)
- If a bully doesn't stop, or attempts to hurt you, they are no longer a bully, they are...

The Wolf

Wolves are trouble, and they generally don't care if you know it. These people are mean and nasty, and they'll try to hurt you to get what they want. Think about a real wolf. When you see them – in the wild or on TV – you can see the intent and aggression in their demeanor.

How to Handle a Wolf:

- Avoid them, by practicing good awareness
- Immediately communicate to someone nearby who can help you
- Call the police, even if you're unsure
- If a situation becomes physical, you *must* defend yourself
- Use any and all force necessary to get away

The Predators

The most dangerous bad guy you can run across is the predator. They are aggressive, violent, dangerous, and – worst of all – they are hard to see. A predator will act like a normal person to get close to their intended victim. This is their camouflage. When they do get close enough, they attack. The predator is often so hard to see that by the time you figure out what they're up to, it is too late.

Examples of Predators:

- Pedophiles
- Con-artists
- Rapists
- Killers
- Child & animal abusers
- Thieves, burglars, robbers
- Anyone who can look and act like a normal person and still commit acts of crime and violence

How to Handle a Predator

There *is* no handling a predator. Remember, they're stalking you, using everyday camouflage to get close to you. By the time you realize there's a problem to handle, you're already in a fight for your life.

Your best bet is to avoid the situation altogether. Thoroughly study the information in Chapter 13, "Understanding the Selection Process." Make yourself as much of a hard target as you can. Also work on threat recognition, and listening to your awareness alarm.

Remember that the predator is counting on you not seeing him coming. If your awareness alarm bells go off, if a red flag goes up, if your instinct kicks in, then his camouflage comes off and you see him for what he is. You don't have to figure out exactly what he's going to do. You don't even have to be sure that he's definitely a bad guy. You just have to know that something might not be right. Then you can take precautions.

If you have a funny feeling, that's enough. Even if you're wrong, you're still alive – so you're also right.

A lot of people are so anxious to avoid confrontation that they refuse to see anything wrong. They'd rather believe that the reason some guy or girl is being exceptionally nice to them is because they're such a nice person themselves. They don't want to confront a predator, so they completely ignore the possibility.

Unpleasant though it may be, you need to realize when you're possibly being set up. Remember, when somebody you just met is being overly nice, gathering too much information on you, wanting to know where you live, offering to take you home when you've had a couple drinks and you don't have a ride – those are red flags.

You've probably seen the stories on the news, where intoxicated women walk off with men they barely know – sometimes several of them – and are found dead the next day. Men, as well. I recently heard of a kickboxer here in Tampa who got into a fight and ended up being found dead in a pond. Just because you're a kickboxer, just because you're a black belt, that doesn't mean you can't be a target for somebody.

The predator doesn't care who you are. As far as he's concerned, there are a million of you. You want to make him see you as a very, very difficult target to acquire, and hopefully he'll eliminate you when he's going through his selection process. That's how you handle a predator.

So, in general, we have these three main types of bad guys – individuals who will approach you aggressively and try to involve you in some type of conflict. That conflict may be mental or physical. It might take the form of an argument with your boss who is always pushing you around, or a schoolyard bully slapping you in the face. It might be that boyfriend who has a glass case over you and is in absolute control of your life, who hasn't laid a hand on you yet but he's mentally abusing you. Or it could escalate all the way up the ladder to the pedophile who stalks children, or the rapist who sneaks into your house at night.

They could be anyone – family, friend, acquaintance, stranger. Whoever they are, they can usually be put into one of these categories of the most common types of bad guy – the Bully, the Wolf, and the Predator – and dealt with accordingly.

There is one other type of bad guy. Fortunately, this type is very rare, but nonetheless they need to be mentioned here.

The Super Threat

The one type of bad guy you cannot adequately prepare for is the psychopath with violent criminal intent (often referred to by law enforcement as the Super Threat). This is the bad guy who walks into an office building and starts shooting at anyone and everyone. They usually don't fear dying, and most of the time they end up killing themselves – but not until after they've done a lot of harm.

Violent criminal psychopaths are responsible for a long list of horrific crimes. These individuals are terrorists in sheep's clothing, and truly deserve to meet their end. A few examples of this group:

- September 11th hijackers
- Virginia Tech campus killer
- Columbine killers
- The Texas mom who killed her five kids in a bathtub
- David Koresh
- Hitler
- Saddam Hussein

This is just a brief list of individuals who don't seem like they're even from the same planet as you and I. There are others out there. Some will remain relatively insignificant. Some will be catastrophic in their actions.

If you have an opportunity to react, self-defense training can be extremely valuable. However, a situation created by this type of individual can be so dangerous that you may not have a chance.

Fortunately, you can also use your training to recognize the potential danger of an unstable person whose life has been changed due to severe emotional trauma, such as lifestyle changes, depression, a medical condition, rejection, or some other traumatic event. If your awareness sends you into an alarmed state in this situation, listen to your instincts, and act accordingly.

The
Basics

"When you drop a pebble into a pool of water, the pebble starts a series of ripples that expand until they encompass the whole pool."

- Bruce Lee, *The Warrior Within*

I think this passage is about being a great human being. What he describes is exactly what will happen when I give my ideas a definite plan of action. Right now I can project my thoughts into the future. I can see ahead of me. I dream. I remember that practical dreamers never quit. I am not easily discouraged; I readily visualize myself as overcoming obstacles, winning out over setbacks, and achieving impossible objectives.

Bruce Lee is well-known for his martial arts movies, especially "Enter the Dragon." But his acting career was just the tip of the iceberg with this magnificent warrior. He only lived into his early 30s, but he was college-educated, he was a phenomenal philosopher, and he was a great father. As a martial artist, he fought uphill battles in the early days just to get martial arts education into the public eye. He went against the grain. He spoke the truth. I am honored to even quote him in my book.

Bruce Lee's words are absolutely timeless.

CHAPTER 11

Two Lessons Pay Off – a Christmas Story

The following is a true story, based on detailed accounts from all the participants involved.

Eight-year-old Sean had always wanted to do martial arts. He'd watched the movie *The Karate Kid*, and he wanted to take karate lessons, but his family couldn't afford it.

Two days before Christmas, Sean came across a TV program that featured some guy in a blue uniform conducting a martial arts class. To Sean, it was the most incredible thing he'd ever seen. So while all his friends were out playing baseball, Sean was in front of the TV, doing martial arts.

Very excited, Sean watched the same program again the next day. He spent Christmas Eve practicing over and over the moves that the guy on TV had shown. They were very elementary lessons, but he remembered every detail.

This year Sean and his little brother Jason had a brand new stepfather, named John. The boys didn't really like John, because he was a raging alcoholic and very aggressive.

Sean and Jason went to bed around nine o'clock on Christmas eve. At approximately one o'clock, Sean woke up when John came into the boys' room, screaming at the top of his lungs. "How dare you! How dare you guys take these toys from the Christmas tree and put them in your bed?"

John was obviously drunk. He reeked of alcohol. He was in his bathrobe, screaming and kicking at the side of the bed.

Sean didn't remember getting up and putting toys into his bed, but as he looked around, he noticed a big blue plastic corvette about three feet long, and a big black plastic truck, with bows on top.

Jason, who was only four, was staring at Sean in disbelief. Jason began to cry.

Sean realized what must have happened. John had been drinking all day. In his drunken stupor, John must have put the toys into the boys' bed and then completely forgot that he did it. So later, when he came in and noticed the toys, he became enraged.

"So who's first?" John asked, still shouting. "Who wants to get spanked first?"

"Not me! Not me!" Jason cried, terrified. "I don't want to get spanked!"

Sean quickly realized that he wasn't going to be spanked – he was going to be in a fight. He knew what was coming, because this guy had done this to both boys before. John didn't just spank; he actually punched and kicked.

John started in with paddling Jason. Then he reached over and grabbed Sean and shook him, and pulled him up by his right arm. He didn't just paddle Sean. He began to punch him in his thigh, push him around, and give him the whole tough guy attitude.

"What are you going to do?" John taunted. "What are you going to do? You're taking toys – these toys that we worked hard to buy for you guys. I can't believe you!"

Sean understood punishment – being spanked for something you did wrong, like lying, or not doing your homework. But this wasn't punishment. This was an all-out fight. This guy might as well have been a schoolyard bully, kicking and punching him. The only difference was, John was much bigger than some kid. Nothing about this was fair.

Sean thought fast. He remembered his first two martial arts lessons, which he'd started watching only two days earlier. He remembered distinctly the guy on TV saying, "The worst thing you can do when somebody's trying to hurt you is nothing at all."

Sean grabbed a book. He hit John square on the nose with the hard spine of that book. He hit him three more times after that, but he couldn't tell if any of those blows landed as well as the first one. But apparently it was enough.

John fell to the floor, mumbling incoherently and holding his nose, blood running through his fingers. Still mumbling, he got up into a chair that was in the boys' room. He tried to say something, then leaned over onto the armrest, and went to sleep.

Meanwhile Sean and Jason ran into the living room, where they eventually fell back asleep.

John didn't wake up until nine the next morning. He didn't remember anything that had happened. He assumed that he'd injured himself by running into the corner of the wall, or passing out and falling on the floor.

That morning, Sean and Jason told their mother what had happened. Unfortunately she wasn't much help to them, because she didn't believe the story. But Sean knew that by grabbing the book, he'd changed the outcome of his situation. Here we have a child who got one piece of information, which paid dividends just two days later.

It's unfortunate that this grown man was an alcoholic, and did something awful to these children. But the point I want you to get is that the older child, having the knowledge and capability to do something to protect himself and his little brother, decided to act. As a result, both boys lived to fight another day.

Any time you learn something – even if it's one line from a guy on TV – you never know when it's going to pay off.

Now let's take this lesson, and let's build upon it.

C H A P T E R   1 2

Conflict Avoidance

The first and most important thing you need to understand about self-defense is that **if you avoid a conflict, you automatically win.**

You can often tell when a conflict is about to arise. It could be a stare-down at a night club. It could be somebody eyeing you or going back and forth in front of you in traffic, making you think that maybe a road rage situation is about to occur. It could be an argument you're having with someone which is growing more and more heated.

When you find yourself in a situation like that, make no mistake: You don't have to step into a ring. You don't have to win a belt. You don't have to win a gold trophy. Whether you rip somebody's head off and kick it down the street, or you run away when someone attempts to rob you at an ATM, the outcome is the same – you win.

That being said, there is also a time to fight. Our C.O.B.R.A. Self-defense Program prepares people to fight in any situation and to win at all costs. But it also teaches conflict avoidance. This is super important.

Say you're at an ATM, and somebody pulls out a knife. They're about six feet away. They're probably not going to throw the knife at you – unless they're one of those circus performers who can throw a knife and hit you on the fly. Can it happen? Absolutely. Anything can happen. But it's highly unlikely. In real life, when somebody is six feet away and they have an edged weapon, the only way that they're going to hurt you is by closing the distance.

If somebody pulls out a knife and says, "I want your wallet, and I want it now!" you have a couple of options. You can stand there, reach for your wallet, and present it to them. Or you can simply run the other way. That's conflict avoidance.

Remember, this criminal doesn't want to get caught. When you take off, he would have to run you down with a knife in his hand, and catch you, just to threaten you again to try to take your wallet. Why risk it? Instead he's going to wait for the next sucker to come up to the ATM and take *his* wallet.

In that scenario, space creates an opportunity for conflict avoidance. It's really important to understand, however, that the entire situation will change in a heartbeat if he walks up to you and grabs you, puts the knife on your throat, and asks you for your wallet. Your options then will be seriously limited, and you need to be prepared to respond accordingly.

But if you can avoid conflict, you should absolutely do so.

CHAPTER 13

Understanding the
Selection Process

A good way to avoid conflict is by understanding the selection process that bad guys generally use to pick their victims.

In nature, predators can be found wherever there is opportunity to catch prey. That's the key: **Opportunity**. This word must be driven into your head. Thoroughly understand that you are most often selected because you present the best opportunity. This concept is so powerful that understanding it can save your life.

I've seen countless demonstrations of opportunistic hunting on Discovery Channel or National Geographic, and you probably have as well. A herd of gazelles are drinking water at a riverside, when in the blink of an eye, a fifteen-foot crocodile leaps up seemingly out of nowhere, and pulls the closest animal in. Why? Opportunity.

How long do you suppose the crocodile was lying low and waiting? Until he saw an opportunity. Then he carried out his plan.

I illustrate this basic principle using the animal kingdom because it's easier for the average person to relate to. Why? Many people, believe it or not, can't comprehend humans having this killer instinct, or predatory nature. Even though we see it daily on the news, it's not taken seriously. However, most people can relate to this behavior in animals, because it's non-threatening to us and therefore doesn't send us into a state of denial.

There's an old saying: "The truth will set you free." Confront your fears, and the death of fear is imminent. When you become educated in personal safety and self-defense, you can put your mind at ease with a well-founded sense of security, instead of pretending that it can't ever happen to you. This is priceless!

So now let's talk about the selection process as it relates to two-legged predators.

People are naturally lazy. It's basic human nature. People, for the most part, will do the least they can to achieve a goal. Criminals especially are notoriously lazy. That's why they steal and break our laws in the first place, instead of going out and getting a job like the rest of us. And that's why they operate on the basis of opportunity.

Example number one – Pretend for the moment that I'm a bad guy. I'm walking down the street, and today I've decided to carry out a purse snatching. I see two females. One has her purse slung over her left shoulder, just hanging down by her left side. The other has the strap over her right shoulder, then it crosses her body, and the purse is on her left hip.

I can run up to the one with the purse hanging straight down, take the purse, and keep running. The other one, who has the strap around her body in a diagonal all the way down to her left hip, presents much more of a challenge. Getting her purse is going to require a lot more effort.

As a bad guy, I'm notoriously lazy. I don't want to work any harder than I have to. Not only that, I don't want to get caught. I don't want to end up in a fight on the street with this woman if I don't have to. I want to grab the purse, and I want to go, before somebody has time to call the police. Bottom line.

So which female would I select? The one who has the purse hanging straight down on the left side, where I can take it and run. Which would I likely eliminate as a target? The other female, who has her purse more secured. Once again, I don't know either one of them. But I will select one and I will eliminate one, based on the opportunity that I see.

Example number two – I'm the bad guy again, and this time I'm perusing the mall parking lot. I'm looking to steal a wallet or a radio, so I'm checking all the car door handles.

Locked... locked... locked... *unlocked.*

It's pretty easy to see which vehicle I'm going to focus my attention on. The one that's unlocked. Why? Because it's broad daylight, and if I have to break into a car it's going to take longer. I might have to smash a window. If I smash a window, somebody might hear it and call the police, or the mall security might come over. Then I have to run for it, and I might get caught, or somebody might get my tag number when I'm leaving.

The car that's unlocked – that's an outstanding opportunity. Very easy. I open the car, I get in, I take what I want, I close the door, and I casually walk away. No one's going to think anything of it, and I get to carry out my plan with little risk of being caught.

In both these examples, easy opportunity equals victim. It does-n't really matter who you are, who you know, or what you're about; ultimately it can happen to any of us. The goal is to make it so dif-ficult to victimize you that you aren't selected as a target. Or if you are, the bad guys can't complete their desired task, whatever it is.

What you want to do is put up hurdles in front of the bad guy. The more hurdles an individual has to jump in order to carry out their plan, the less likely they are to pick you. They're going to eliminate you as a target because you're not "falling behind the herd."

Think of building a wall. This is another easy concept to under-stand and apply. Since the dawn of time, a wall has represented a secure boundary. Walls, fences, doors – these are all barriers. Even at the movie theater there's a rope to keep you in a line. All of these represent boundaries, security, and order.

Your job, as a person interested in developing the ultimate personal safety and self-defense mindset, is to aggressively apply this idea of creating obstacles and boundaries to your daily life. Think about this until it becomes second nature.

T.P.M. =
Time – Place – Method of Attack

An attacker will always have the initial advantage, because he starts off with control. He or she will almost always have complete control over what time they attack. Once a time has been selected, they will choose a place that's convenient for them to carry out the attack. Last but not least, they will choose the method of attack, or the means with which to physically harm you.

You, as an honest and upstanding citizen, won't have the luxury of knowing in advance the time, place, and method of attack. Usually the plan is in full swing before you're even aware of what's going on. In most cases, you won't even know your attacker – his history, his strengths and weaknesses, or anything else about him.

What can you do to counteract these overwhelming factors? You must become vigilant about your time and place, so as to not present yourself as an easy target (opportunity). Constantly ask yourself these critical questions:

Where am I? – What time is it? – Who am I with?

This, above all else, can lead to total conflict avoidance. An attacker will quickly target or reject you based on where you are, what time it is, and who you are with.

Scenario A: It's 2 p.m., and you're at work. You're with two to five coworkers, talking, working, and so on. You remember you left your cell phone in your car, and you run out to the parking lot to grab it.

Scenario B: It's 9:30 p.m., and you're at work. Everyone else left at 8:30; you stayed late to finish up a small project. You remember you left your cell phone in your car, and you run out to the parking lot to grab it.

If you were an attacker, which scenario would appeal to you more?

Please tell me you answered B. This set of circumstances creates a greater opportunity for robbery, rape, auto theft, or any other crime for that matter.

Scenario	A	B
Time	2 p.m.	9:30 p.m.
Place	with coworkers	alone

That's not to say you *can't* be attacked in broad daylight. Remember, anything is possible. It's a question of putting the odds in your favor. Change your time and place, and you change the potential outcome.

CHAPTER 15

Say It
Out Loud

One of the easiest ways to "link" into our common sense is to state the obvious. Often there's so much clutter in our heads that thoughts can get lost. Speaking something out loud works much better.

Think about it. Have you ever lost your keys? To find them, you probably talk to yourself: "I came inside, I walked over here, then I..." It helps you focus.

Likewise, when you encounter suspicious circumstances, saying all the details out loud to yourself can help you sort things out.

Example 1: You're at work. You go to the lunch area, and your normal group gets a little quieter when you show up. Your guts twist because this isn't normal.

Out loud (to yourself): "When I show up, they get quiet, turn away, and pretend like nothing's going on. They have a hard time making eye contact, and conversation is generic at best."

What does this mean? It could be anything. The key element is that it deviates from a normal pattern.

Example 2: Your friend thinks his girlfriend is unfaithful. You ask why he thinks this, and he states that she's been going out more without him, and is always on the cell phone at home.

Out loud: "She goes out with friends she hasn't seen in a long time for a five hour dinner on a Saturday night. The phone rings and she goes to the other room with the door shut for thirty minutes. She gets nervous and defensive when I ask her questions about any of it."

What does this mean? You don't need to be a genius here. If you say nothing, I think a psychiatrist would say you're in denial.

Do you get it? This is a powerful technique to help you recognize a threat.

Out loud: "There's been a car sitting at the end of the block for the past three days. The windows are tinted, but I can tell there's a guy in it, and he doesn't live on this block."

What does this mean? Possibly someone is scouting your neighborhood to see if there are any opportunities. Robbery, burglary, kidnapping, rape – remember, these are all crimes of opportunity to a bad guy.

Get in the habit of saying things out loud to yourself when you notice something suspicious. It really works.

CHAPTER 16

A.A.A – The Three Phases of Attack

Your first line of defense should always be to avoid conflict by making yourself a hard target – someone who is rejected during a bad guy's selection process. But sometimes, despite your best efforts, "stuff happens." Therefore you need to know how to handle the conflicts that do occur.

Any conflict has three phases or stages: Awareness, Alarm, and Action.

Awareness

During the Awareness phase, you stay constantly alert as to where you are, what you're doing, and what's going on around you. You should be in this stage all the time, in an effort to prevent a conflict from occurring. But your awareness also allows you to realize as early as possible that a conflict is indeed imminent – hopefully before the situation gets completely out of control.

Signs you're in the Awareness phase:

- "Where are am I?"
- "Who is around me?"
- Noting environmental conditions

- Maintaining personal security level
- Looking for suspicious circumstances
- Listening to your gut feeling

Alarm

Once you become aware that something just isn't right, you enter the Alarm phase. Even if you don't know yet exactly what's wrong – or whether there's really anything wrong at all – you enter a state of heightened awareness. This is your body's way of preparing to deal with a crisis. This is also a good time to shift course, and hopefully avoid the potential conflict.

Signs you're in the Alarm phase:

- Feeling that something isn't right
- Recognizing a potential threat
- Thinking accelerates
- Auditory & visual exclusion (tunnel vision) occurs
- Decision-making ability is impaired
- Shortness of breath
- Adrenaline rush (fight or flight)

Action

Now there's no longer any doubt – like it or not, you're under attack. Whether it's a verbal, mental or physical altercation, you have to take action. Your wellbeing is at stake – maybe even your life. Whether or not you're prepared to respond appropriately and effectively will determine the outcome of this situation.

Possible responses to the Action phase:

- Physically remove from situation
- Defend

- Panic/paralysis (fear/giving up)
- Attack
- Counterattack (instinctual)

Once you've entered into any of these three phases of self-defense, your mind and body are warning you that you're now escalating into a possible criminal act or crisis situation. By recognizing a potentially harmful situation in the Awareness or Alarm stage, you can likely avoid the Action stage. Remember, this is your body's natural defense system, so listen to it.

CHAPTER 17

Combat Conditioning

Let's talk about how real-life combat actually affects you.

A lot of our students are prime athletes. They run daily, or they have some other exercise regimen, and they're in peak physical condition. But when we run them through a real-life scenario – say a simulated carjacking, or robbery, or home invasion – within thirty to sixty seconds they begin to shut down physically. They're panting like they just ran five miles, or played a full game of whatever sport they're involved in. And it was only thirty to sixty seconds.

Why is that? Why is a conditioned athlete not able to take that fitness and transfer it into reality combat conditioning?

The answer is adrenaline – the adrenaline dump, the overwhelming fear, the fight-or-flight response that your body is going through.

All the running and all the basketball and all the cycling and all the spinning and all the cardio classes in the world can't prepare you for what your body is going to experience in a real altercation. It's going to shut down. This is very important to understand.

In the C.O.B.R.A. Defense Program, we train diligently on counteracting this physical shut-down by getting students used to the adrenaline. Adrenaline inoculation training includes an instructor screaming instructions, and putting you through attention diversion drills. You also have a bad guy dressed in pads, and he's steering you left and right, grabbing, holding – sending you into the unknown. Being able to fight through this is so very important.

Now let's talk about the trained martial artist.

If someone has a lot of skill, but hasn't experienced real-time training – that adrenaline dump and the fight-or-flight response – they haven't learned to control this reaction. One of the things that adrenaline will do is take the techniques you've learned and trained so diligently on, and throw them right out the window.

Your hands feel like they're gigantic bricks. You feel like you're moving in slow motion, like you're stuck in the mud. It's the bad dream syndrome: "I can't move. I'm stuck in the middle of the street. Nothing's working. I'm hitting the guy and it doesn't hurt him."

That's what adrenaline does. It makes your vision fuzzy. It shuts off your hearing. It makes it seem like you're looking through a straw.

We have a home invasion drill that we do, in which a student goes through a series of events, including attention diversion drills. They're striking shields and bags. They're engaging a bad guy. They've got to open a locked door and go through, then shut the door and relock it. All these different tasks simulate an actual home invasion.

In the middle of this drill we shout out a color. We yell it right in their ear as they pass us. At the end we ask the student, "Do you remember your color?" The first time students do this drill, nine out of ten times they have no idea what the color is. They're just happy they made it through.

We had a class in which we had several experienced martial artists, as well as several police officers. And there was a distinct difference between the police officers, who have had the real-life training, and the martial artists, who have trained in a static atmosphere. Striking shields and pads and even sparring are done in a controlled atmosphere, which doesn't lead to the fear that is involved in a realistic experience. It makes a distinct difference.

Even some of the law enforcement officers had a challenge with this drill. They couldn't remember their color. You're going through this entire scenario, and you're confused, you're panicked, and it feels very, very real even though you're in a controlled environment in our facility. Your mind is your worst enemy at this point, because it shuts everything else out to focus on the threat that's right in front of you.

After doing this drill several times, the same students not only remember the color, they can remember every move they made, every strike they threw. When did they end up on the ground? Where was the bad guy standing when they approached him? They can recall all of this.

What this kind of training provides is clarity in combat. The fog begins to lift. Your mind stays in control in spite of the body's physical reaction to what's going on. You've created the ability to focus in actual real-time combat. This is priceless.

Raging Giants – Fear and Pain

Fear and pain can serve and drive a person effectively. However without proper training, mindset, and courage, these two can destroy and paralyze a person before the outset of an actual event.

Harness your daily fears – of the unknown, and those caused by scars from your past – and use them as fuel which enables you to overcome anything.

Why would you, an individual striving to strengthen their warrior spirit, care to waste valuable seconds of your life contemplating fear and pain?

Pain and fear are one in the same. They feed each other and help each other grow. Pain is a physical response to bodily harm. Fear is an emotion in response to something that doesn't even exist. It's a premature reaction to an unknown circumstance. This is the equivalent of a mental prison. Your body suffers while you ponder the unknown outcome of a situation that may or may not happen.

If your worst fear comes to pass, there's nothing you can do except deal with it. It was supposed to happen exactly like it did, or it wouldn't have happened like it did. Does this make sense to you? You can't stop it. You can't change the future or what's supposed to be. So fear is actually a giant raging monster that we not only created but feed and keep with us at all times. This is pointless and a waste of the only life you will ever get. Focus, train your mind, and realize you can drive a sword through that monster you call fear.

Verbalization and Command Presence

Communication is key. Whenever you want someone to know something, do something, or respond to you, you must communicate with them. How else will you get your point across? You won't. Nobody knows your intentions unless you tell them.

The same is true if you are ever attacked, assaulted, or threatened. Do you think your attacker will stop if you talk nicely to him, or if you say nothing at all? Absolutely not. He'll only become more confident in what he's doing.

Never think that the bad guy is fearless, because that's the furthest thing from the truth. Criminals use intimidation as a weapon because it makes their job easier. But inside, they are just as afraid as you are. So when you start yelling "Help!" "Get back!" or "Stop!" the bad guy panics, because you've messed up his plan. Criminals are notoriously unorganized and lazy, and this guy probably doesn't have a "Plan B." At this point, chances are good that he'll decide to cut his losses and run.

All this yelling also draws attention to the situation, which might attract help. People have been abducted and killed, and no one heard a word. Why is that? If someone is trying to take you somewhere you don't want to go, you'd better scream as if your life depends on it – because it probably does.

Another way you can help yourself in an altercation is by developing **command presence**.

Command presence is the assertiveness you convey when you're put on the spot. Think of someone you know who is an effective parent, teacher, or coach. You might refer to them as "a natural leader" because they quietly project inner strength and confidence. You know who they are and what they want.

You might have a hard time imagining yourself having "command presence." But the more you learn about personal safety and self-defense, the more confident you'll feel. And you'll find that you won't have to go around telling people about it. They'll be able to see it – and so will the bad guys. It's one more way you can trigger their fear and give them second thoughts about messing with you.

Don't be afraid to let the people around you – especially the bad guys – know you mean business. Verbalize, sound off, and have a command presence. It can save your life.

CHAPTER 19

What Can Hurt You?

I was once told to stare somebody right in the eyes if I really wanted to know their intentions. Maybe you've heard that same advice at one time or another.

Bad advice can get you killed.

While it's true up to a point – you *can* determine a lot about someone by feeling somebody out, and trying to discover truth or deception – you can also get lost trying to stare into someone's eyes. You lose your peripheral vision.

What makes an individual dangerous? Number one it's their arms and hands. It's their ability to throw objects, or strike you, or hold you down and choke you, or use a weapon.

I would never jump into a tank with a great white shark. Why? Because it has powerful jaws full of sharp teeth. What makes a great white dangerous? The fact that it can bite your leg off.

Now if someone were to pull all those teeth out – *all* of them – I'd no longer be afraid to jump into the tank. What made the shark dangerous is no longer there.

Now, suppose you have an attacker in front of you, and he has no arms. How afraid are you? Probably not very.

Can he hurt you? Absolutely. He could throw a kick. He could hold you down with his legs and bite you. But he's going to be ninety percent ineffective with whatever he does. Why? Because he can't grab you, or punch you, or wield a weapon. You're going to be able to pretty much dominate this individual.

So when you're talking to a person, watch their body. I've never been struck by somebody's eye. An eye has never flown out of somebody's head and hit me, and until it does, I'm not going to lock onto the eyes as though they're going to hurt me.

Hands hurt you. Elbows hurt you. Knees hurt you. Weapons hurt you. People blading their body, shifting their weight, bringing their hands above their waist – these are signs they may be about to hurt you. Somebody's eyes will not hurt you. I can't be more simplistic than that.

CHAPTER 20

False Bravado, or "Tough Guys Eat Cotton Candy"

I want you to create a mental picture of a bad guy. Make him the scariest bad guy you can imagine, right out of your worst nightmare.

Maybe it's a 15-year-old gang banger with a gun. Or maybe it's the guy in the dark alley, wearing a long, black trench coat and holding a bloody knife. Or maybe it's the 250 pound bald guy with a goatee, who's got piercings all over his body, and prison tattoos on his arms and his neck and the side of his head. Whoever he is, he's walking tough, he's oozing bad attitude, and you just know he means to hurt you.

Does this guy scare you? Would you want to fight this individual?

If you create a vivid enough picture of this guy in your mind, you'll actually start to feel the fear. You'll feel the adrenalin pumping, and your motor skills shutting down, and everything else that goes along with being afraid.

At this point, you may be worried about what will happen if you ever do run into a guy like this in real life. How can you possibly defend yourself against somebody like that?

Often we can't fight back the way we want to because we give our opponent too much credit. Believe it or not, this is one of the biggest obstacles people have to overcome when in a self-defense situation.

Why do we give them too much credit? Because we don't know them. But guess what – they don't know you, either. That's a really important concept to understand.

Don't just focus on the other guy. Also think about what's inside you -- the knowledge you've learned, the skills you posses, and the confidence you have to use them. Often the battle is won or lost inside your own mind.

Let's say a 12-year-old is approached by a 25-year-old man who wants to abduct him. What the child is afraid of is the size and apparent ability and authority of this much larger person. If the child doesn't understand that he could gouge this guy's eyes out, bite him, kick him, scream, yell, and throw objects at him, and by doing those things be able to save himself nine out of ten times, then that child is going to be terrified, and he'll go into shut-down mode, which will leave him vulnerable.

Same thing with a female. If you're a female you might not be able to defend yourself against a large male or a group of females that approach you, say outside a nightclub. But the truth is, you can – if you know how.

Now, let me qualify all this by saying that you always want to assume that the person you're going to meet up with is going to be tough and mean and possess the ability to possibly take your life. To do otherwise would be foolish. To go around believing that you can beat anyone and everyone without even trying would be asking for trouble. But to give this person superpowers when he doesn't deserve them would also be foolish.

Often what you see is nothing but false bravado – a swaggering pretense of courage. It's the image a bad guy projects in order to instill fear in people. Remember, the kind of bad guys we're talking about here use intimidation as their chief weapon. They don't want to fight any more than you do, so they try to scare you so badly that you'll shut down and be unable to do anything to stop them from carrying out their plan.

What can you do to take this weapon away from a bad guy?

Your body feels the effects of fear, but it's your mind that creates that fear. I once heard someone say that the word fear stands for "False Evidence Appearing Real." In other words, when a bad guy projects an image of being tough and mean and deadly, it's your belief in that image that instills fear in you.

So the first thing you need to understand is that the individual who would attack you is a human being. Don't build them up to be more than they are. Don't give this person more credit than they deserve. Don't give them more strength, more intelligence, or more skill.

Inside, they're the same as you. They have the same doubts, insecurities, and concerns that you do. They have a history. Their confidence can be broken. They will tire. When you cut them, they bleed red. They *can* be defeated.

The second thing you can do is to take your visual image of the bad guy you're facing, and strip away all the scary parts: The tattoos, the piercings, the dark clothes, the bulging muscles, the tough expression – all of it. Mentally take all that away from them, stuff it in a little box, and throw it in the lake.

Anybody can wear flashy armor. The medieval knights believed that the fancier their armor, the more intimidated their enemies would be. Other warriors put on war paint for the same reason. But again, it's all about what's between your ears. Someone with low confidence and a lack of knowledge will be intimidated by what they see on the outside. But now *you* know better.

It's just like public speaking. You've probably heard the advice, "Picture the audience in their underwear." Why? People are a lot less impressive when they're sitting there in their boxers, or a bra and panties. You give yourself a psychological advantage.

When I'm facing off with someone, I strip away everything

visible on the outside. I change what they're saying into baby cries. And last but not least, I put cotton candy in their hand, just like at the carnival. To me this cotton candy represents innocence – someone who is child-like.

So visualize this with me: Now the individual who is standing in front of you isn't some bad-ass who got off his motorcycle and walked up to you with a wallet on a chain, and tattoos, and sunglasses, and a nasty attitude; he's a pathetic kid in his boxers, crying, with cotton candy in his hand.

When you do this exercise, it doesn't have to be cotton candy. You don't have to strip them down to their boxers. But you need to use whatever image works for you to bring them down to where they look insignificant to you. That's the first step to overcoming and beating someone – stripping away their false bravado.

Yes, you're going to be in a fight for your life. Yes, you're going to fight harder than you ever have, and take this seriously. What you're not going to do is give them power that they don't deserve.

And yes, tough guys eat cotton candy.

The Martial Arts

Lack of Knowledge

Doubt creates fear...
fear paralyzes the mind...
the mind controls the body...
the body responds to action –
or it doesn't.

Fear, doubt, and lack of control are the byproducts of lack of knowledge. To kill and destroy what paralyzes us, we must become very familiar with it – whatever it may be.

CHAPTER 21

The Difference Between Martial Arts and Self-Defense

The difference between martial arts and self-defense training is a huge subject. In general, the two are completely different – and yet they are exactly the same. This is a hard concept for many people to understand. Since I'm both a martial arts school owner and a self-defense instructor, I completely understand the differences. But many do not. Many confuse the two.

This confusion may stem, at least in part, from the fact that in the beginning, martial arts and self-defense were one and the same.

Although some are more recent, many martial arts have been handed down for hundreds or even thousands of years. They were developed in a time when laws were minimal and wars were common. Feudal lords battled each other for territory. Empires invaded other empires. Bandits marauded unchecked. Those who wanted to survive had to know how to defend themselves, by killing other human beings when necessary.

In other words, martial arts were the original "self-defense."

Further, there has been no new technique or move created for thousands of years. We shouldn't pat ourselves on the back for "creating a new way." People give the techniques different names. They may teach them differently. They couch them in different philosophies. However, nothing truly new has been taught in many lifetimes. You can call the same punch ten different names, but it is still the same punch – the same lock, the same choke, the same take-down, the same basic maneuver.

This may surprise a lot of people, because today we have so many different martial arts. We've all seen so many different things on TV and in movies. But these differences aren't in the techniques themselves – they're in the delivery.

These differences in teaching and presentation are actually a great thing, because it exposes so many different people to self-defense and martial arts. But we must come to the basic under-standing that the martial arts were created many, many years ago, out of necessity, because the warriors of old had to use them in real combat.

Today, many martial arts focus on sport. Sport, by definition, includes knowledge of one's opponent, a preset time and place, no deadly weapons, time limits, safety equipment, points, prizes, titles, referees, fair weight classes, and many other rules.

Not that there's anything wrong with sports. The martial arts in particular emphasize the long-term pursuit of physical and mental excellence. If your goal is to be a point tae kwon do stylist, you'll want to train to be good at point tae kwon do. If you're going to be an MMA cage fighter, you need to train for that. If you work hard and you're good at whatever sport you choose, you're going to win a lot of trophies, and you can feel good about that. But understand that they are sports.

Here's an example to think about: Sport and self-defense are as different as:

• going to the gun range and shooting targets (SPORT)

– and –

• being in an actual shoot out (REALITY)

Again, there's nothing wrong with being a target shooter. The mistake is made when a target shooter thinks that a real shootout is going to feel the same as shooting in a safe, controlled environment. But it isn't the same at all. Targets don't shoot back – and that makes all the difference in the world.

Can you die in a sports-oriented martial arts match? It's possible. Anything is possible. But please understand that when two people go into a sparring match, they generally enter this competition expecting that they will most likely survive. There might be some performance anxiety, but there is not what we call primal fear – the kind of fear that will shut you down and completely erase all your techniques.

If you've trained only on the level of sport, without an added element of reality, when primal fear hits, everything you've learned will go right out the door. Your mind has to get used to real-life scenarios. Without that, the training doesn't link when it's carried over into a real-life situation. It doesn't matter how much you hit a bag, or break boards, or condition your body – if you've never experienced a fight realistically in your mind, the link isn't there, and the training has poor carry-over.

A real-life fight is nothing like a martial arts competition. Throughout my law enforcement career, while working in corrections, and during my many years participating in the martial arts and being a teacher, I've had a lot of different real-life experiences. In none of those situations has anyone ever tried to get me in an arm bar and tap me out.

When two skilled individuals meet, it's a test of skill, conditioning, knowledge of your opponent, knowledge of the rules, and knowledge of your limited environment, whether it be the mat or the cage or what have you. However, someone with a lot of skill is generally a well-kept and disciplined person. They're not out there looking to start a fight with you in some parking lot. So when you get into a real-life situation, for the most part – ninety percent of the time – your opponent, though aggressive, is going to be highly unskilled.

That doesn't mean they can't hurt you. But this lack of skill leads to a lack of general knowledge of reality. They might be over-confident, which is disastrous if they meet someone who actually *is* skilled.

People always say, "Hey, all these fights go to the ground." Well, generally the two people who get into a brawl are unskilled individuals, so it's going to go to the ground, because that's all they know. I have a three-year-old, and he will tackle you. I didn't teach him how to do that. It's basic human nature to grab somebody and try to take them to the ground. So when two people meet who have no training and no background, then yes, they end up on the ground.

A skilled individual can get you on the ground, keep you on the ground, and hurt you on the ground. Or they can hurt you standing up and keep you standing up and not get taken down. That is a major, major difference. Skilled versus unskilled – skill wins.

So how can you make your martial art skills translate to real life? Your brain must get involved. The biggest muscle you have – the biggest weapon you have – is that thing between your ears called your brain, and you have to use it.

It's tremendously important that you view your brain as a computer. As I mentioned before, it needs to create a "link" from your martial arts training to reality self-defense.

Have you ever clicked a web link, only to end up on an error page? That happens because the link is "broken." The necessary information isn't there to get you where you want to go.

Likewise, if you're a trained martial artist, your body has all the skills you need to defend yourself; but if your brain doesn't make the proper connection, all you get is an "error message." Your brain shuts you down or distorts your skill set when it encounters something new and unfamiliar.

That's why, to be effective, self-defense training must include stress inoculation and frag drills, auditory and visual exclusion training, attention diversion drills, and real-life (professional) scenarios. Robberies, burglaries, attempted rape, battery, bullies, weapons – all these can be simulated in training. This gives your brain the "link" it needs to put your excellent martial arts skills to use. It's what makes your skills "battle ready."

This is why self-defense instruction today is often completely different from a martial arts program.

Please understand that there are so many martial arts that I can't speak for all of them. But generally martial arts have a hierarchy, which includes a master instructor and assistant instructors, and students who are ranked according to a belt system, with the black belt being the most senior. The focus is on discipline, form and tradition.

In a self-defense program, you often have more of an academy-type atmosphere. Generally, the protocol of a martial art is set aside. You have general respect, but there is no bowing, no "yes sir" and "no sir." Instead of the traditional martial arts uniform (called a gi), students are wearing a t-shirt, shorts and tennis shoes. And the focus is on learning effective techniques that students can carry outside that day and use immediately.

When you walk out the door after a self-defense class, you might not be in any better shape, and you may not have been studying for years, but you have something you can use right away. Something that if you're in the mall, or walking out to your car, or you go home, and someone attacks you, you can immediately use it. In situations like that, you don't have time for years and years.

Now, the ideal training is the self-defense program that moves into a martial art. This is outstanding, and you really want to look for this when you're looking for a program. Then you can have the best of both worlds. But you have to know the difference between the two, and make sure your training takes reality into account, if you want to be able to use your skills to defend yourself in a real-life fight.

I'm very simplistic in talking about self-defense versus martial arts, and its application in reality; but I want to be super simple, to drive the point home.

The Story Behind the Black Belt

In the old days, the longer you practiced, the dirtier your belt would become. You started off with a white belt, and it eventually got darker and darker, until finally it turned black. Hence the most senior student is called a "black belt."

CHAPTER 22

Experienced Martial Artists and the Warrior Mind

Are you willing to endure great physical pain, impose even greater pain upon another person, and ultimately take a person's life in a combat situation? Will you be able to do this when you must without it conflicting with your view of yourself as a moral person? I truly hope you can, because if not, God help you.

If what I just said stirred you up or got you to say something like, "He's out of his &#@% mind!" then I have done my job and moved you a little bit. If you already carry a true warrior spirit, then you probably didn't skip a beat.

I have the utmost respect for true martial artists or self-defense practitioners, regardless of their chosen system. If you spend your hard-earned money and your valuable time training for physical and mental security and excellence, then you deserve the respect of your peers (if you're respectful toward others and humble about yourself).

However, realize that if you fail to understand this principle of the warrior mind, your training and experience will educate you and get you in great shape – and yet ultimately be useless in combat.

Assuming that you're an upstanding, moral person, the human being who would initiate conflict with you does not in any way deserve an ounce of sympathy during the progression of active combat. Your purpose should be to avoid, defeat, overcome, and – if you must – kill anyone who would attempt to take you from this world. Combat can be ruthless, and there is absolutely no room to be a tree-hugging bleeding heart who doesn't want to hurt anyone.

Let me be perfectly clear: You don't have to be Rambo to adopt this mentality. You could serve fries at a fast food restaurant and be a pure warrior; it's all psychological. By having intensity of purpose in combat, you can rest assured that you will still be standing after even the most violent storm.

Your motivation:

- Family
- Friends
- Experiences
- Possessions
- Money
- Adventure
- Happiness
- Life
- Opportunities

A warrior's mindset (intensity in combat) will protect these at all costs, whether it's a verbal, mental, or physical altercation.

CHAPTER 23

Philosophy: Five Principles of Martial Combat

Combat is physical conflict involving violence, generally between humans, usually as part of warfare. Combat may be armed or unarmed. It may take place under a certain set of rules, or be unregulated.

To achieve success in combat, one must master these five principles of martial combat:

1) ***Discipline*** – Training to accomplish a certain task or to adopt a particular pattern of behavior, even though one would really rather be doing something else.

When relating Discipline to Combat, it is necessary to realize the best course of immediate action, while simultaneously ignoring all other distractions. This course of action will be the most effective and efficient, and it will be carried out with absolute resolve. Discipline does not ensure any sort of victory or security for a person. It only reinforces your training and resolve.

2) ***Attitude*** – Manner, disposition, or feeling with regard to a person or thing.

When relating Attitude to Combat, your body must adopt the

intensity of purpose that you posses in your mind. An adversary can see and pick up on your strength, will, and knowledge, or lack thereof.

Your posture, eye contact, movement, voice, and all your other body language must absolutely display what the mind has formulated: PURE CONFIDENCE. This type of attitude in combat sends a distinct message that you are willing to go through anything to avoid or overcome another in any situation. Impose your will, your training, and all that is in you to wage war and overcome in any conflict. This can represent itself in any form of combat, be it physical, mental, verbal, emotional, business, or any other situation involving two sides.

> *3) Presence* – Dignified manner or conduct; the ability to project a sense of poise or self-assurance, especially before an audience.

When relating Presence to Combat, realize the true definition, which is *command presence*. Appearing bigger by projecting your presence in a situation creates tremendous tactical advantages. Understand that appearing bigger really has nothing to do with actual physical size. Think in depth about this and it will be understood.

> *4) Respect* – Esteem or high regard for a person; acknowledgement of the worth or excellence of a person.

When relating Respect to Combat, it refers solely to you, not your adversary. Developing martial respect for yourself cultivates and empowers the warrior's spirit and belief in your ability. Respecting yourself in this manner will allow you to win all battles, whether physical or not, and keep you from losing that which is most valuable to you.

5) Mushin – A Japanese word that translates "mind/no mind"; a state of being conscious but without thought.

When relating Mushin to Combat, or to life in general, it should be understood that you must have an unobstructed mind. This mindset strongly reinforces confidence and proficiency in all tasks.

Mushin is one of the hardest mindsets to achieve; however, it yields the highest rewards and creates the greatest opportunities for success.

Iron Mindset – Attaining Mushin

Sit quietly for as long as you can without cultivating an active thought or memory. Do not think of colors, music, activities, or words. Think of absolutely nothing and simultaneously be very aware of your current environment. This exercise is incredibly difficult, and at first it will take about ten seconds before you lose control of your mind and a thought enters. Time this exercise as many times as possible.

Your goal is to reach one minute of absolute nothingness. If you attain this goal, go for three, then five minutes.

In Japan, this is called Mushin. I also like to think of it as Absolute Focus.

If Mushin is attained for a full five minutes, you have gained control of your mind. You now control a mind that has been on autopilot since birth, easily influenced and overwhelmed. Your goal is to eventually be able to achieve this focused mindset no matter where you are or what you're doing.

When you can truly attain Mushin, understand that you have developed an iron mindset capable of achieving and overcoming all challenges.

Keep in mind, this is not meditation. You don't have to sit and close your eyes. However, in the beginning it helps to limit your distractions. It will come to you in short bursts, then leave as fast as it came. Keep practicing.

Religion plays no part in this whatsoever. It's about being a focused warrior and human being. To have control – absolute control – of your mental state is to have great power as a person, despite the life you lead. Many of history's greatest leaders and thinkers achieved at the highest known levels by harnessing their absolute focus, or Mushin.

Beyond the Basics

"This is a strong Warrior attitude: Extend your energy above and beyond the enemy's body and spirit. Never cringe in fear and never fight without your spine being straight. This indicates your resoluteness to go in hard and cut the enemy down. You first beat the enemy with your spirit and then you beat the enemy with your hands and your sword. Go for the kill with utter resolve and commitment."

– Miyamoto Musashi, *The Book of Five Rings*

Musashi had over sixty confirmed kills in his lifetime, before the age of thirty. He was a Samurai his entire life, and I would venture to say we may be able to learn something from his writings.

In this translation, "spirit" is confidence, and "hands and sword" means skill set. Confidence and skill set will overcome in emotional, mental, and physical conflict. What are you doing today to make this happen? What have you done in the past? The point is to train very hard, and believe in yourself like no one else will.

CHAPTER 24

Your Motivation to Train

By now you should know that you can receive life-changing benefits from taking even a basic self-defense class or seminar. But maybe you've read this far, and having seen how what you've already learned can help you, now you want to know if there's more. Say you don't have a background in martial arts, but you want to take your training to the next level. Where do you start?

If you want to develop a true warrior spirit within yourself, you're going to have to put forth some effort. Achieving excellence in any endeavor takes hard work, and this is no exception.

To succeed, you need motivation. Motivation to go out and sign up for a class. Motivation to stay on top of your personal safety. Motivation to keep improving your physical ability to defend yourself in today's society. You need something that inspires you to stick with it, even when you get tired, or bored, or distracted.

Everybody's motivation is different. What I'm going to do in this chapter is create an outline for you to live by, and you're going to fill it in with the details of your life.

You're standing in a room. Behind you is a safe. It's the biggest, strongest safe in the world, and you're the only one who knows the combination. Nobody in the entire world can get what's in that safe unless you open it for them, or give them the combination. Not the best thief in the world, not the toughest person. They have to go through you.

You remember that picture we painted earlier, of the toughest guy in the world – the guy with all the false bravado? That guy – your biggest fear – is now in that room with you. He wants to know what's in the safe.

Here's what's in that safe: The top three things you value most in your life. Number one should be your actual physical wellbeing and life, because without that you can't have anything else. Number two would be every person you care deeply about – family, friends, and loved ones. (Or if you prefer, you can detail it down to the one person you love the most.) Number three is maybe your favorite material possession.

Picture these three things in as much detail as possible. In fact, put down the book now and don't continue with this chapter until you have put those three items in that safe, and you're very detailed and specific about them.

Do you have it? Is the safe full?

All right. You have the combination in your head, and you also have it written down in your back pocket. Your biggest fear just walked into the room. He wants it. What's going to happen now? Are you going to just give it to him – or are you going fight?

He asks you for it, and you tell him no. He slaps you in the head. What do you do then? He pushes you to the ground. What do you do?

You stand up. You become angry. But he's intimidating you. You've built him up to be bigger than he is. What do you do?

You strip away his false bravado, you take his confidence from him, and you destroy him. You don't let him take another step.

Why? Because what's in that safe matters to you, and you know that nobody on this earth has a right to take it from you.

You can do this mentally as well as physically. Remember, this book is not about going out there and just flattening someone with your fist.

Your opponent might be that boss at work who is intimidating you, giving other people raises over you, not appreciating your hard work. And then you step into her office, because right now she is your biggest and toughest bad guy. And you have the training and you have the heart and you have the will to confront her. You eliminate that lump in your throat, and you stand there, and you look at her squarely, and you stare right through her. You make her understand that she will never get that combination. Ever. You'll die first. You're willing to fight tooth and nail, to the end, verbally, mentally, and physically.

When you do that, the individual standing across from you will be able to feel your confidence, your energy, and your absolute resolve. And that will affect what they try to do to you.

If what you put in that safe is dear to your heart, then you will take this chapter, and thoroughly understand that the motivation you need to do what you need to do has to come from somewhere. And it's in that room, in that safe.

CHAPTER 25

How to Train for Maximum Effectiveness

Although it might be admirable to do so, you don't have to live on a mountainside and train like an ancient samurai warrior twenty-four hours a day, seven days a week, to reach a reasonable level of proficiency in self-defense. However, knowing how to train for maximum effectiveness is very important. In this chapter I'm going to show how you can train as efficiently and effectively as possible, at whatever level you choose to pursue that training.

There are many different ways to learn something. You could attend a seminar, read a book, watch a video, and/or attend a formal martial arts class. There are many different classes you could take. You could work at it for a day, a week, a month – or you could do it for a lifetime. It's up to you to decide what works best for you.

There are basically four different levels at which you as a student might approach learning martial arts/self-defense. These are:

- The novice
- The hobbyist
- The professional
- The serious practitioner

All of these levels are valid, and how far you choose to progress is mostly a matter of personal preference and degree of interest.

If you're reading this book, you already fall into one of these categories.

- **The novice** – *"I don't know anything about this, and I'm trying to get information."*

You know it would be a good idea to learn how to defend yourself if the need ever arises, so you pick up a book or watch a DVD. Maybe you attend a weekend seminar or training camp. You learn some handy tips and techniques you can use in your everyday life to make yourself less of an opportunity.

- **The hobbyist** – *"I enjoy this, so I'm going to spend my free time getting deeper into it."*

Now you're taking classes one or two nights a week. You're practicing the physical skills to gain proficiency. You've moved beyond the novice level, but you're still pursuing it part-time, as a hobby.

- **The professional** – *"I do this for a living."*

You have (I hope) worked hard to develop your skills in martial arts, self-defense, stranger awareness, or safety education to a level where you're qualified to teach others. You consider this your profession, and you pursue it accordingly. You get paid for your efforts, either as an instructor, or running your own business. (This level may or may not overlap with the next level.)

- **The serious practitioner** – *"This is who I am."*

This one, to me, is the top of the pyramid. You don't have to own a school to be a serious practitioner (although you can). You don't have to make a dime. You just have to take it seriously. You practice it daily. You think about it daily. You work hard, on your body and on your mind. You're putting yourself mentally in situations as an exercise. You're finding out how self-defense and martial arts can bring peace, flexibility, and longevity – can improve every aspect of your life. You seek out knowledge, you're very open, and you have no ego. You are the serious practitioner.

8 Techniques to Increase the Effectiveness of Your Training

It doesn't matter if you're a novice, a hobbyist, a professional, or a serious practitioner – if you use these eight techniques that I'm going to share with you, you can progress in your training much faster – in some cases reaching your goal years sooner – than the average person who doesn't use these techniques.

(By the way, these techniques can also be used outside the realm of self-defense and martial arts. When you understand them, they can be applied to many areas of your life.)

1) *Hear it.* Don't just listen passively to what the instructor is saying – really hear it. There's a big difference. You need to make sure you truly understand what you're being taught.

2) *See it.* Some people are auditory learners, and some people are visual learners. Seeing a demonstration of a technique imprints a picture in your brain, which reinforces what you just heard.

3) *Do it.* Try it for yourself. Literally go through the motions. This also helps you to internalize the skill. Don't worry if you're awkward at first; you'll get better with practice.

These first three techniques are as far as most people go. If you stop here, your progress will be average. If you want to maximize the effectiveness of your training, however, put the remaining steps into practice, as well.

4) ***Drill it.*** You need to put in some time. You need to break a sweat. Make it real for yourself. Drill on a bag, in the air, with a partner. They say it takes up to 10,000 repetitions of something to create muscle memory. Ten thousand may sound like a lot, but you can do it in a relatively short amount of time if you're moving at a reasonably fast pace. And once you build that muscle memory, your body never forgets. And that's when you begin to really learn.

5) ***Write it.*** This is huge. Writing something down makes it real for you. Hearing something is fine, but when you write it down, you're mentally programming it in your brain. If it's a certain kind of punch or kick, or a move, or a technique – write it down in your own words, because your words mean more to you than anybody else's. Once again this reinforces everything else.

6) ***Practice it.*** Get out of that static environment where you're drilling in a classroom or with a friend. Take the initiative to practice on your own, alone, without being told to by somebody else. This reinforces your training.

7) ***Rehearse it.*** Mental rehearsal is something I can't preach enough. Build a scenario in your head, and go over and over and over it. Maybe you're getting out of your car, and some guy comes up to you, and he's asking for your wallet. Or he's just asking for directions but you feel uncomfortable. What would you do? Maybe you're tackled to the ground by someone trying to take the money you just got out of the ATM machine. What technique

would you use? Maybe you're out late at night and someone who is intoxicated comes up to you and becomes verbally abusive. What would you do? Remember, we've discussed how your mind doesn't know fact from fiction. Make it real for your mind, and it becomes real for everything else.

8) Teach it. Find somebody else who wants to learn these skills, and try to teach them what you've learned. This is the ultimate reinforcement. It's been said you don't really understand something until you can explain it clearly to someone else. Just be sure you diligently go through all the other steps first, and you've got it down. Passing on incorrect information is embarrassing for you, and could be dangerous for them.

No matter what level you're working at, whether you're a novice, a hobbyist, a professional or a serious practitioner, you can use these techniques to improve the effectiveness of your training.

If you're a serious practitioner, drilling or practicing on your own might involve four hours every day of intense training – working hard, sweating, only stopping to drink a glass of water and eat a meal. If you're a novice it might be doing a few moves three or four times each on a Saturday afternoon.

Either way, you did do it. And that means you're getting the most out of what you've learned, and making serious progress toward your personal goals, whatever they may be.

Threshold Training

The human body is a remarkable machine capable of many extraordinary things. However, our mindset and beliefs will sometimes keep our bodies from reaching even half of what they're capable of.

Understand that whatever mental limits you place on yourself, your body can easily soar past them. It all comes down to want. You have to want to reach physical excellence in your chosen path. You don't have to attain greatness to become what you desire. You just have to want it, and that will lead you to it.

Break down your mind and body to a point where "quit" enters your mind. When this happens, keep training at a level 10 for another five minutes. This will be the toughest five minutes of your entire life, and you must resolve to shed all thoughts and pain that hold you back. Take everything, every thought or emotion, and push it over a cliff. Say good-bye to it. You're now a different person.

Complete this, and you will then understand threshold training and the rewards it holds.

CHAPTER 26

Self-Offense

It's long been a mistake to think of self-defense training as purely self-*defense*. To be defensive means to prevent attack. To not get hit. To not get hurt. To find an escape route. To protect your physical body.

A defensive tactic is, "He did this, and I did that, so I didn't get hit. He pulled a knife, so I grabbed the knife, and I took it from him; I stopped a knife attack. I stopped someone with a firearm. I stopped someone from punching me. I kept myself from getting hurt."

As we've discussed earlier in this book, you should avoid trouble whenever you can. Preventing a fight is as good as (or better than) winning one. But establishing a training regimen with this mentality exclusively can ultimately be a flawed tactic. Let me explain why.

Defending against an attack is enough only about fifty percent of the time. Hurting another individual comes into play more often than you might think.

Self-defense alone, without the additional mentality of self-*offense*, is like playing a sport to not lose. A football team that shows up just hoping not to lose inevitably has a hard time winning. You have to be prepared to actually overcome something. And sometimes the only way to overcome something is by going through it.

Let's say a 23-year-old man named Joe is walking out of a night club. He accidentally bumps the shoulder of a man who happens to be intoxicated. This man then follows him outside. Joe, practicing self-*defense*, keeps walking. He tries to ignore the drunk man, but the man taunts him and pushes him from behind.

Joe creates space. He uses command presence and asserts himself. He says he doesn't want anything to do with this. He doesn't become aggressive. He apologizes. He does everything he can to avoid further trouble. Finally he even runs, but the man, and now his friends, run after him. They corner him outside by his car.

Now Joe is backed up against his vehicle with up to three subjects in front of him. (He might actually have only one aggressor here; the guy's friends might only be onlookers. But it doesn't matter. It could be one on one, it could be one on three. Either way, Joe is pretty much out of options to avoid getting into a fight.)

This individual (Joe) who is up against his car being assaulted, has tried every outlet he possibly can to avoid this situation. He's already tried to talk the other guy down, and it didn't work. The guy is aggressive, he's intoxicated, and he's looking for a fight. Now the mindset of self-offense has to kick in. For Joe, the only way out of this situation is through the aggressor(s).

If he only has a defensive mindset – if he's never thought about offense – he's in trouble. He's not prepared to think, "I have to hurt this person. I have to stop the threat."

Sometimes that's what it takes. Not just a punch. Not just a kick. Because the aggressor picked the time, place, and method of attack. He won't stop until you make him stop. Who decides when a conflict is over? Not you. You have to fight one hundred percent from start to finish, until your opponent quits.

How long will that take? You won't know until it's over.

It's the equivalent of running a race, and no one told you how long the race is supposed to be. Are you running a hundred yard dash? Or are you running a mile? It could be a 5-K, it could be a 10-K, it could be a marathon. It could be a triathlon! You don't know.

Not only do you not know, you can't care. You just have to keep going. You have to be extremely offensive to win in these situations.

That's why when you think about self-defense, you have to include offensive strategy, as well. If you're going to keep yourself from getting hit, you also have to be able to deliver enough pain and punishment to another individual – or several individuals – in order to stop the threat.

Stopping the threat is the only thing that matters. If some guy pulls a knife and he's attempting to stab you, you might have to shoot him. That's stopping the threat. If somebody pushes you, one punch might knock him down so you can run. That's offensive tactics, and that's stopping a threat.

If someone is threatening you verbally, and you walk off and get in your car and drive away, that may be enough. The incident is now over. You stopped the threat. But relying on defensive thinking only is a flawed tactic. There will be situations where you run out of defensive options, and you must be able to think offensively as well.

So how do you learn to think offensively?

Believe it or not, most people aren't naturally aggressive. They don't want to hurt each other. Hurting someone is a learned skill. It's something you have to train for.

In our C.O.B.R.A. Self-Defense organization, we train students from all walks of life. One of the things we do is put them into realistic scenarios with a realistic bad guy. We might role play a car jacking situation, or an ATM robbery, or a home invasion. If they've had little or no experience with hitting anything, they have a very hard time being aggressive toward this individual.

Keep in mind, our "bad guy" is dressed in head-to-toe padded gear, so he can't really get hurt. We've told the students that the rules of engagement allow them to hit this person. They can hit him in the face with open-handed strikes, they can grab and knee-strike, they can punch and kick. And yet invariably, many people will half-heartedly hit center of mass on the bad guy.

The bad guy could be in somebody's face, yelling and scream-ing, "What are you going to do?! What are you going to do?!" The instructor is behind the student saying, "Hit him in the face! Hit him!" And yet many of our students, in the beginning, will only hit the bad guy in the chest, when they're allowed to hit him in the face – when in fact they've been *told* to hit him in the face.

Even when you give the student a training weapon, like a fake gun or knife, they won't use it. Because people are good by nature, and acting offensively is a learned skill. Striking another human being is a learned tactic. It has to be "brought out of them."

You might be thinking, "Well, I would hit him in the head!" But until you're in that situation, it's very hard to relate to it. And many of our students find that what I've described here is exactly what they do in the first couple of weeks of their training academy.

By the end of their academy, they're striking from head to toe. They've become more aggressive, in a productive and healthy way. They've learned the tactics they needed to learn to actually protect themselves in a real-life situation.

Here's another example of a situation where being able to think in terms of self-offense as well as self-defense might be critical.

Let's say someone breaks into your house. You're not alone; your spouse or partner is there – but that doesn't help. Two indi-viduals come in and order you at gunpoint to go into the bedroom, while they keep your wife or your husband in the other room.

Now you're in the bedroom with one bad guy, and your spouse is in the other room with another. Your bad guy tells you to turn around and face toward the wall, and get down on your knees. Then he starts rummaging through your dresser, looking for valuables to steal.

Apparently he finds holding a gun at the same time awkward, so he puts the gun down on top of the dresser. Out of the corner of your eye you see that the gun is just within your reach.

At this point you might be asking, "Would a bad guy actually do this?" They do it all the time. They're not the most intelligent people. Once again, they think you're so petrified you're not going to move.

So you see the gun within reach of your hand, and you go for it. Now *you've* got the gun. Do you have what it takes to act offensively and shoot this individual, and then go to the other room and shoot the other one? Maybe you do, and maybe you don't – but this isn't the best time to find out.

Say they don't have a gun. Say it's just a knife. But you have the same situation where they split you and your partner up into different rooms. And you find an opportunity to not only take the knife, but to engage this person in hand-to-hand combat. Do you have what it takes to stab him, or to latch onto his neck and squeeze until he's no longer moving? Do you have what it takes to kill him?

These people are in your house. They just split the two of you up. God knows what's going on in the other room with your spouse or partner. And God knows what they have planned to do at the end of their robbery. Maybe they'll leave you to call the police, and you'll live happily ever after. Or maybe they'll kill you execution style. Do you really want to wait around to find out?

When you train in a self-defense program, the course should include self-offense. They may not call it that, but you want to make sure you're getting a complete program. Self-offense training includes heavy amounts of striking, reality-based striking, and conditioned combative responses.

Once again, do you have what it takes to take another person's life in order to save your own? That's an important question to ask yourself – before your life depends on the answer.

Right Below the Surface

Be nice in life. Be very nice. However, be prepared to kill anyone you meet until they give you a reason not to.

This will give you a demeanor that acts as a bullet proof vest for your mind, and thus for your body as well. If you embody and understand this, you will have taken a giant step toward cultivating a cutting-edge mindset as it pertains to self-defense and martial arts training.

There is no certain "type" you need to be to develop this way of thinking. It doesn't make you mean, angry, or paranoid. You don't walk on egg shells, and you don't fake anything. But for anyone who would pose a threat to you or your family or your way of life, it would be like running full speed through a mine field while being shot at and on fire. It would be a very bad day for them – and they wouldn't know it until it was too late.

You can smile, have fun, and relax. Meanwhile, right below the surface there's a serious warrior.

Strive to attain this.

CHAPTER 27

Conditioned Response

What's a conditioned combative response? Allow me to share a true story with you.

Back in the 70s and 80s, law enforcement officers who had been killed or wounded in intense shootouts were often found to have empty magazines buttoned back in their holsters. The obvious question was – why? Why had they taken the time to take a piece of metal that was no longer useful to them in combat, and refasten it in the holster?

When I was a law enforcement officer, I was told about a study which uncovered the answer.

Back then, officers were trained on the police department gun range, under non-stressful conditions. When officers finished shooting at a target, they would eject the empty magazine, put it back in the holster, and button it back up. And nobody had ever thought anything about it.

But then when the officers were out on the street, emptying their weapons at a bad guy, they would automatically take the time to release the magazine, put it back in the holster, button it, and then get another one out and reload. In other words, in the heat of battle, this individual was doing exactly what he had done at the police firing range, because that was the way he'd trained. He didn't know anything different.

Today, police instructors teach the opposite. You push the release, and you let the empty magazine fall to the ground while you reload. You pay no further attention to it. Your whole mission is to get ammunition into that weapon as quickly as possible. But this lesson was learned the hard way.

So how does this apply to self-defense?

The topic of conditioned response to training is enormous. It's an entire book in itself. What you need to remember is that how you train is exactly how you will react under stress.

Say you're training in an intense environment, hitting a punching bag with everything you've got. You've put a face on that bag, you've developed a situation in your head, and you've made it very real for yourself. And then as soon as you're done punching, you drop your hands to your sides. Now, if you're ever in a real fight, you'll punch somebody and then drop your hands to your sides. Without even thinking about it. Because you will fight exactly like you train.

If your training is watered down, if it's unrealistic, if it doesn't serve a purpose in reality – when a real-life situation comes knocking at your door, you'll have nothing to draw from. But when you link your self-defense techniques to reality, you reach a point where you don't have to think about what to do, you just do it. This allows you to use the adrenaline rush to give you superhuman ability – you're hearing better, you're seeing better, you're faster, you're stronger. That's very important.

Here's another story about conditioned response, and how individuals respond to a stressful situation.

Our C.O.B.R.A. students do a drill in which they run from a cone to a bag about fifteen feet away, and strike it. Then when they hear "Retreat!" they're supposed to run back to the cone. When they hear "Weapon!" they're supposed to pull their training weapon and point it at the bag. When they hear "Fight!" they're supposed to put the weapon away and run to the bag again.

In this particular class, the instructor was yelling "Weapon!" and "Fight!" and "Retreat!" over and over and over, and one of our students got stuck in what we call a "goofy loop," or hypervigilance. Basically that means your brain locks up and doesn't know what to do. And when you have no idea what to do, you do the first thing that comes to mind. That isn't necessarily the best thing, or the smartest thing. It may not even relate to the situation. This happens quite often; I've seen many different variations of this in our training.

In this case, the student took the weapon, and instead of pointing it and pretending to shoot, he threw it at the bag. The stress of the situation had developed in his head to the point where he just locked up, and did the first thing that came to mind. And the first thing that came to mind was throwing a rubber handgun at a bag, and yelling at the top of his lungs. (Clearly his conditioned response needed a little bit of work!)

Let me give you one last example of how training doesn't always translate very well when you first use it in any kind of real-life situation or conflict.

I distinctly remember my first arrest. I had recently completed approximately seventeen weeks of training in the academy: listening to all my instructors, learning my use-of-force matrix, taking state tests and having to answer every question right, practicing skills over and over again in a law enforcement training environment. We'd done hundreds of simulated arrests, using real handcuffs and practicing on other students. All this training built our confidence. "Hey, I can do this," I thought. "I can arrest somebody."

My first real arrest involved a domestic situation. We'd separated the couple, and I was building my probable cause. I remember feeling my heart pound – and that was just from the decision-making process I had to go through. I had this long list of questions scrolling down the screen inside my head. "Do I have the probable cause?" "What's the state statute for this?" "Did I read Miranda?"

"Did I do this correctly?" "When do I know it's the right time to take this person's freedom?" "Oh my goodness, I'm going to take this person's freedom!"

Keep in mind, I had spent seventeen weeks preparing for this. I should be ready, right?

I had enough probable cause. My field training officer was looking at me, saying nothing, waiting for me to make the decision. And I made it. On the outside I was very cool, calm and collected. On the inside I was a mess. I was asking myself a million questions, because I was doing something for real for the first time in my life, as opposed to doing it in a training environment.

Now that I look back on it, the transition went fairly smoothly from how I trained to what I actually did – mostly because the guy didn't put up a fight. I asked him to turn around, and he did. I told him, "Sir, you're under arrest for domestic battery." I put the handcuffs on appropriately, and I took him in. But I wasn't as calm on the inside as I would have liked. And if anything would have happened that required me to make multiple decisions, or if I'd gotten into a physical conflict, my first arrest might have turned out quite differently. My training was good, but I still wasn't used to the stress of a real-life situation.

The most valuable thing I learned from the first arrest in my law enforcement career was that I learned more in that thirty-five minutes in a real-life, on-the-job situation than I did training forty hours a week for seventeen weeks in the police academy.

Real experience pays off. Real experience stays with you. And you can build upon real experience. Which is all the more reason why your training needs to be as realistic as possible.

Conditioned responses to combat must be an integral part of the way you think, how you train, and what you look for when you seek out professional self-defense instruction.

BOOK 6

The Journey and the Calling

"Fierceness is essential in mortal combat. It is never dependent on the amount of destruction you wish to bring upon the enemy. There must be no hesitancy in using any method to bring about the complete and utter destruction of the enemy. It is the only way to ensure victory of a lasting nature."

— Sun Tzu, *The Art of War*

Once again, this lesson is applicable not only to training and actual hand-to-hand combat, but to business and relationships, as well. Basically what Sun Tzu is saying here is that procrastination can kill you. If you decide to hit someone but you're in fear, and you don't do it, that might be the deciding factor. If you're going to cross a major highway and you go one, two, three steps out, and then you hesitate, you might get hit by a car.

Once you move, you must go forward with utter resolve. When somebody says "go" at the start of a race, you don't jog, and look to your left and your right to see whether or not everyone else is taking this seriously. You take off like the fastest person on the planet. And whatever the end result, you know that you gave it your best.

Do not hesitate – ever.

CHAPTER 28

The Journey and the Calling

Whatever path you decide to follow when it comes to self-defense, safety, and the martial arts...

Whether you're the novice, the hobbyist, the professional, or the serious practitioner...

... you're going to take a journey. Along the way you will build a road that can take you absolutely anywhere in life.

This is something you can't fully understand until you do it.

I've been building this road for myself my entire life. It's what I do. It's what I know. I've spent my life studying, and later teaching, self-defense and martial arts. I've been in combative situations in law enforcement, as a juvenile boot camp instructor, and working with mean, vicious, high-priority felons in a correctional environment. I've also taught average adults and children in a professional martial arts setting, and through seminars. I've developed the C.O.B.R.A. Self-Defense Program.

This is the path I've chosen to take.

Following this road helps you in every area of your life. It keeps your physical body in shape, improves your flexibility, and adds to your longevity. It lessens stress, improves your thinking, and increases your motivation. It helps your creativity. It helps you sleep better at night. It gives you confidence. It provides greater security, not only for you but for those around you.

This is no little dirt road in the woods. It's a giant highway upon which you can get anywhere that life wants to take you. Following it really will lead you success in work, in relationships, and in raising your children. It will take you on a journey that you can't possibly imagine – one you have to experience to understand.

I also like to think of every martial artist, in the beginning, as raw material. However seriously you take this journey, you are raw material, and your finished product is going to be an immaculate, gleaming weapon. It will have the ability to kill, and it will also have the ability to attract. It is of immense value – sometimes even priceless. And it takes time to make, but once it's made, it is cherished by those who posses it.

A samurai sword is an absolutely beautiful weapon and instrument. It can be hung up for decoration. It can be given as an award. It's cherished as an historic relic. The samurai sword is an almost indestructible weapon created thousands of years ago by people who had to use them on a daily basis. So the samurai sword is a phenomenal analogy for the individual who will choose to take this path in training.

The raw material that goes into making such a sword is just a big pile of nothing in the beginning. You wouldn't recognize what it was if you walked by it on the street. As a matter of fact, you'd probably clean it up and throw it in the garbage.

A master craftsman will take this raw material, and heat it, and hammer it until it begins to take shape. Then it's put under even more stress – heated up and stretched out and folded, pounded and beaten, then plunged into water and cooled – over and over again, until it transcends its humble beginnings and you can begin to see what the outcome of all that hard work will be. By the time he's finished, that sword is razor-sharp and gleaming, arguably one of the finest weapons ever created.

As a student of martial arts and self-defense, you can choose to stay in that raw form. Or you can choose to be transformed into this samurai sword. The master craftsman, in this case, is the instructor, or book, or other source of knowledge which forges you into a shining example of what you can be, and what you can learn, by taking this journey, this lifelong journey that is so enriching and so rewarding.

Once you become this weapon, once you have this skill, once you become this instrument that can not only put people in awe but also devastate someone with one blow, you can never take it for granted. You have to keep the blade sharp. You must never let it rust. You must never let it get dull. You must never let it collect dust.

The journey is about making that sword, and then keeping it sharp by never letting your skills and your knowledge fall to the wayside and become ineffective. You work so hard to get to the point where you are that samurai sword. You need to work just as hard to keep the blade sharp.

In closing, if you have not already sought out a self-defense program or seminar, or a martial arts program, I highly advise you to seek out whatever program best suits your needs. If you don't like the first program you try, you can change to another one. There are so many great styles out there, and so many great instructors, people on the cutting edge, willing to teach these things. You just have to have the want and need to learn it.

Having that mindset for survival – understanding that you can prevail and overcome in any kind of conflict or situation – holds more value than anything else on earth or high up in the heavens. Knowing that you can control your destiny, and support those around you with the knowledge that you've learned, is priceless. I hope this book has supplied you with the information you need to take a giant step forward in that direction.

High Ground

As a martial artist – or whatever your chosen talent or field is – always fight for the high ground. High ground means "tactical advantage in whatever you're doing." Your years of study and practice will reveal the high ground. Take this advantage with absolute resolve.

Sensing an advantage or opportunity of any type, you must take the high ground without hesitation, and fight to keep it. The harder and longer you train, the easier it becomes to attain and keep this tactical advantage known as high ground, in any endeavor.

A Good Start

I would like you to write down fifty things you can do immediately to increase your personal safety and improve your self-defense. The list should be specific to your life and family. This may seem challenging at first, so here are some ideas to get you started:

- Lock car doors as soon as you get in, and drive off immediately
- Keep a light on when you're not home
- Install flood lights
- Travel with friends
- Take a self-defense class
- Don't run alone at night
- Install a home security system
- Keep windows locked
- Carry your purse in front of you
- Always leave five to eight feet between your car and the car in front of you
- Park under lights
- Keep unknown people in front of you
- Speak with assertiveness
- Understand pre-attack indicators
- Lock doors
- Never mix alcohol and strangers
- Do not brag about possessions
- Do not count money at an ATM
- Avoid drive-throughs late at night (from 11:00 p.m. on)
- Understand and know how to use everyday weapons
- Understand that a cell phone can't help you
- Realize that even if you have a gun, you probably can't get it out in time

• Watch for occupied unknown cars sitting in your area
• Listen to your gut – always

Kid Specific:

• Keep backpacks on one shoulder, not two, so that it comes off quickly
• Never put names on backpacks where people can see
• Travel with two or more people
• Keep lines of communication open
• Enroll in self-defense or martial arts class
• Learn that bad guys can look nice, and don't be fooled
• Understand that kids ages 5-12 cannot punch or kick their way out of a situation
• Become familiar with anchoring and anti-kidnapping techniques
• Never be on foot at night

This list can go on for pages and pages. Each one is a wall or obstacle which a bad guy will have to overcome to get to you. You can get further information about this at:

www.cobradefensesystem.com

under "Personal Safety and Self-Defense."

Resources

Recommended Reading

The Book of Five Rings, by Miyamoto Musashi

The Warrior Within, by Bruce Lee

The Art of War, by Sun Tzu

Living the Martial Way, by Forrest E. Morgan

On Killing, by Lt. Col. Dave Grossman

Lone Survivor, by Marcus Luttrell

The Truth about the Martial Arts Business, by John Graden

Websites

http://www.cobradefensesystem.com

http://www.cobradefense.com

Here you can find lots of free information and articles about self-defense, as well as links to all C.O.B.R.A. Self-Defense System products and services, including those listed below.

C.O.B.R.A. Self-Defense System Training Academy

- Survival skills
- Close quarter combat
- Escapes
- Strikes
- Scenario training drills
- Weapons
- Assertiveness
- Confidence
- Deadly force situations
- Psychology of defense
- Stranger awareness
- Anti-abduction skills

C.O.B.R.A. for Adults

A 10-week academy (2 nights per week).
Includes:
- Orientation
- Training Manual
- T-Shirt
- Graduation Certificate

C.O.B.R.A. for Kids

A 6-week academy (2 nights per week), for kids ages 7-13.
Includes:
- Training Manual
- Parent Handbook
- T-shirt

Fight For Success Series –

Professional and Personal Development
by Chris Sutton
- *Goal Setting*
- *Overcoming Adversity*
- *How to Have More Energy, Less Stress, and a Better Attitude*
- *Creating the Ultimate Body*
- *How to Start a Business*

For more information:

Write to us at 24103 U.S. Hwy. 19 N., Clearwater, FL 33759
Call us at 1-888-531-7375 or 727-791-4111
Email us at info@cobradefense.com
Visit us at http://www.cobradefensestore.com

Chris Sutton is a professional martial artist and reality combat instructor, with over 20 years of training and teaching experience. He has worked tirelessly to increase awareness of personal safety issues. His belief in the need for reality-based self-defense training for all ages was a huge inspiration behind his creation of the C.O.B.R.A. System, a cutting-edge self-defense program which has benefited a wide variety of people, from stay-at-home moms and retirees to martial artists and professional law enforcement and military personnel.

Chris has earned numerous black belts in both the Chinese and Japanese martial arts systems. He also studied under world champion kickboxer Jim Graden, and, with further influence from legendary champion Joe Lewis, earned another black belt in the Elite Kickboxing System.

As a member of N.A.P.M.A. and a certified A.C.M.A Coopers Institute Instructor, Chris is a lifetime student of professional self-defense and martial arts instruction, philosophy, and continuing education.

Summary of Additional Professional Qualifications:

- Former certified law enforcement officer for city/county agencies
- Former corrections officer
- Former law enforcement drill instructor
- UBC instructor
- Chief instructor/owner of the United Martial Arts Academy
- 15-time gold medalist in the Florida State Law Enforcement and International Law Enforcement Olympics
- Creator of the C.O.B.R.A. Self-Defense System
- Creator of C.O.B.R.A. for Kids

- N O T E S -

- N O T E S -

TO ORDER MORE SELF-DEFENSE
PRODUCTS/INFORMATION

Including:

- Videos on basic/intermediate/advanced self-defense techniques
- Technique books
- Child safety books
- Audio books
- Miscellaneous products
- FREE reports
- To schedule a seminar

Contact us:

Online: http://www.CobraDefenseStore.com
http://www.CobraDefenseSystem.com
http://www.CobraDefense.com

Telephone: 888-531-7375 toll-free, or 727-791-4111
(For product orders, have your credit card ready.)

Email: cobradefense@aol.com

By Mail: CES Publishing
Chris Sutton
24103 U.S. Hwy. 19 N
Clearwater, FL 33759

NEW!

Take the COBRA Self-Defense
10-Week Academy online!
For more information, visit

www.SelfDefenseCollege.com

– OR –

To become a certified
COBRA Instructor,
take the online course at

www.SelfDefenseCertified.com